Routledge Revivals

The Foundations of Political Theory

First published in 1958, *The Foundations of Political Theory* strives to answer essential questions of politics by studying its foundations. In this book, Mr. Greaves treats the state as only one among several associations whose function is to promote entirely human ends. He tries to reinterpret such ideas as 'self-realization' and the 'good life' in ways acceptable to students of contemporary philosophy, who reject the theological and metaphysical doctrines these ideas have been tied to in the past. He insists that men get their moral standards and their ideas about what makes life worth living by reflecting on their experience; that there are no ultimate and self-evident moral principles. While admitting that moral standards are subjective in the sense that we cannot explain how men come to have them except by showing how they serve their needs, he refuses to allow that rational argument about them is therefore impossible. Since men are rational, since they have purposes and ideals and not merely desires, and since they know that to realize these purposes they must live with others, there are moral standards acceptable to all men when their function is understood.

The Foundations of Political Theory

H. R. G. Greaves

First published in 1958
by George Allen and Unwin Ltd

This edition first published in 2022 by Routledge
2 Park Square, Milton Park, Abingdon, Oxon, OX14 4RN
and by Routledge
605 Third Avenue, New York, NY 10017

Routledge is an imprint of the Taylor & Francis Group, an informa business

© George Allen and Unwin Ltd, 1958

All rights reserved. No part of this book may be reprinted or reproduced or utilised in any form or by any electronic, mechanical, or other means, now known or hereafter invented, including photocopying and recording, or in any information storage or retrieval system, without permission in writing from the publishers.

Publisher's Note
The publisher has gone to great lengths to ensure the quality of this reprint but points out that some imperfections in the original copies may be apparent.

Disclaimer
The publisher has made every effort to trace copyright holders and welcomes correspondence from those they have been unable to contact.

A Library of Congress record exists under LCCN: 59000596

ISBN: 978-1-032-18451-7 (hbk)
ISBN: 978-1-003-25460-7 (ebk)
ISBN: 978-1-032-18455-5 (pbk)

Book DOI 10.4324/9781003254607

THE FOUNDATIONS
OF
POLITICAL THEORY

H. R. G. GREAVES

Ruskin House
GEORGE ALLEN & UNWIN LTD
MUSEUM STREET LONDON

FIRST PUBLISHED IN 1958

This book is copyright under the Berne Convention. Apart from any fair dealing for the purpose of private study, research, criticism or review, as permitted under the Copyright Act, 1956, no portion may be reproduced by any process without written permission. Enquiry should be made to the publisher.

© *George Allen and Unwin Ltd*, 1958

*Printed in Great Britain
in 11 on 12 pt Baskerville type
by Simson Shand Ltd
London, Hertford and Harlow*

FOREWORD

THE student of politics asks why he should prefer one kind of political organization to another. He wants to know what a political organization should aim at, and by what criteria he is to judge its ends, its methods, and its achievements. He enquires, too, why he should obey, and if there are ever occasions when he should not. These are not 'improper questions', and they will continue to be asked. Political theory must produce guidance on how to deal with them, or perish. That is not to say that it must be able to provide a simple and clear answer, and only one answer, to every practical problem. But it is to say that political theory must show how we should go about their solution, what is the nature of an orderly proceeding in the matter, what considerations ought to be in our minds, what—in short—are its foundations.

This is, then, to deny the view that political science can only describe behaviour without attempting its systematic appraisal, or that the search for unifying concepts or basic principles for general guidance is mistaken and unprofitable. Yet that view is just what there is a growing tendency in recent years to adopt. Were it to become widespread political theory would destroy itself: it would lose its interest to the lay mind and much of its claim to educational usefulness. That it may not be alone in running this risk is suggested by some remarks of the Regius Professor of Modern History, who is reported as having said, in his recent inaugural lecture at Oxford, that classical scholars had killed the classics and that, unless we take heed, there is a danger that philosophers may kill philosophy, philologists literature, and historians history.

But what follows here is only an introductory essay. It is not an attempt at a comprehensive structure. I am concerned with suggesting why, as I think, guiding principles should be sought, and in what manner they should be sought, not with their application over the whole subject. With these wider developments, which belong more exclusively to political science and public administration, I should like to deal later, in what might be a sequel to this introduction.

It is one of the difficulties of the kind of discussion that I have attempted, and a danger for him who undertakes it, that it must trespass upon the preserves of other specialists. Especially do the foundations of political theory lie in the fields of moral philosophy, sociology, and psychology. That, I hope, will explain my treading these preserves, and my frequent borrowing from those to whom they belong. I can only give this necessity as my excuse, and crave the indulgence for my inadequacies of those whose knowledge of these disciplines is greater than mine.

Finally I should like to express my gratitude to the several friends and colleagues who have given me their very generous help. My debt to Professor Morris Ginsberg is evident and deeply felt. I wish also to thank Professor Karl Popper, Mr Leonard Woolf, Professor K. B. Smellie, and Mr Ralph Miliband, for giving me their time and the benefit of their comments at various stages. Their criticism and encouragement has been greatly valued; but none of them must, of course, be blamed for anything that I say or fail to say in what follows. I thank Miss J. Wallis, too, for all her secretarial assistance.

H.R.G.G.

London School of Economics and Political Science

February 1958

CONTENTS

FOREWORD	page	7
I The State: Definitions		11
II Foundations and Criteria		31
III Purpose		42
IV Obligation and Command		61
V Reason and Political Purpose		74
VI The Individual and Morality		93
VII Sociality and Morality		106
VIII The Content of Morality: Rules and Values		118
IX The Social Good		141
X The State and Social Purpose		156
XI Democratic Political Theory: Applications		172
INDEX		206

I

THE STATE:
DEFINITIONS

ARISTOTLE wrote that the state is a creation of nature, and that man is a political animal, meaning that the state is necessary to his satisfactory existence. Augustine saw the source of the state in original sin, man requiring to live under authority in order that his evil tendencies should be restrained. Thrasymachus regarded the state as no more than the rule of the stronger. For Herbert Spencer, in the time of primitive man the state had not come into existence, and he looked forward to a blessed condition in which the state would have ceased to exist, an eventuality in the anticipation of which Marx shared. Hegel described the state as God walking on the earth, and the British idealist philosopher Bosanquet saw the state as the incarnation of a moral order. The late Lord Lindsay described the state as an agreed way of settling differences.

However we may seek to define the state or to trace its origins, in the actual world we live in we have no difficulty in recognizing the state. Some eighty manifestations of it are members of the United Nations Organization. The characteristics they seem to share are that they are groups living on, and exercising control over, a definite territory. They are divided into government and subjects. Some sort of system of order is represented by each. Rules of law are established and in some measure maintained, and compulsion is exercised, the right to it being recognized both by the members of the group and by the outside world. Clearly then the state is some form of association with some special characteristics, particularly that of its territorial connection and of its use of force.

And the questions in practice which we need to ask about the state relate particularly to this matter of compulsion or force. We need to ask about it indeed the question which we should ask about any association: what is its purpose? How is this attained? And what are the obligations which the pursuit of it entail upon its members? Problems in connection with its use of force should properly arise as matters subsidiary to its purpose, justified by relation to it. It has happened, however, that this possession of supreme coercive power has seemed to many to be so clearly the essence of the state that they have regarded power as the end or purpose of the state, and not as the means with which it is endowed for achieving the results for which it exists. But this is surely to put the cart before the horse. For rational enquiry must clearly demand of any organization to what it is directed and what human needs it serves. It is true nevertheless that power is so germane to the state that most political considerations will necessarily find some basis in it, and many relate solely to how it is exercised. And it has often enough happened that the state has been treated as though it were the only possessor of power or of 'sovereignty' unlimited, unquestionable, and inalienable.

But that such a picture does not correspond to the facts becomes immediately apparent when we look at the state in the context of other states, and of other associations.

Although it was the case in the past that for most purposes many states could act as though no others existed and they clashed only at such distant margins on the far off periphery of their authority, that condition no longer prevails today. The state in the world of other states is restrained by all manner of limitations upon its exercise of power. First there must be borne in mind the whole complex power structure of the world community. This restricts at innumerable points the free exercise of power. That such freedom varies between the small or weak country, in terms of economic and military resources, and the so-called great power was indeed recognized in the very constitution of the United Nations Organization; for here we find that the requirement of unanimity in many important matters applies only to those few states which are permanent members of the Security Council, and the rest may be overridden by a majority. Even among the great powers there are few indeed which in practice can afford to 'go it alone'. There is no need to labour the point that strategic considerations, that is the weighing of conditions of military and economic strength, enter into the making of nearly all elements of foreign policy, that is policy concerned with any matters of inter-state relationships. But there are other restraints upon the exercise of state power. International law sets important practical limits. Although in the last resort this may depend upon the application of sanctions about which there is uncertainty as to whether they will be or can be exercised, there is a large area of activity in which questions are never pushed to any such ultimate resort. While states, it is true, largely make international law and regard themselves as bound by it only when they have given their assent to it in the form of treaties, not only does law as thus embodied in treaty form as created in the past act as a restraint upon the freedom of the state in its international relations, but the law itself embodies principles or directives which are the fruit of custom, or reflections of ideas of equity generally accepted. And again here it clearly acts as a restraining force upon state freedom. There is, moreover, an influence having comparable effects which is constituted by international public opinion; and this has on many occasions been given expression to, significant illustrations of this being provided by the assembly of the United Nations, the assembly of the League, as well as by many technical and specialist agencies. Although again this force has often been flouted, and in the last resort may have only uncertain sanctions behind it, there can be no question either of its existence on many important occasions or of the restraining force that it continually exercises. Thus we may say that international institutions by organizing and expressing such opinion may both increasingly bring elements of compulsion to bear that restrain the liberties of action of the state and may also, through the provision of advantages secured to conforming members of international society, encourage activities which otherwise the state in the free exercise of its power would not have adopted.[1]

The state, looked at from within, has its activities subjected also to many restraints. These again may be set by the facts of

[1] Further see J. H. Herz, 'The Rise and Demise of the Territorial State', *World Politics*, IX, 4, pp. 473–493, who deals with the effects of economic, psychological, air, and nuclear force on the basic concepts of the modern state system.

power. There are groups, organized bodies, and unorganized interests within every state which limit its operations. Moreover it may be said that although the state largely makes the law there are often basic principles of law, or nationally accepted customs, or even prejudices of opinion, which set restrictions upon the free exercise of the state's coercive authority. Especially when these express deep convictions or firmly held moral judgments do they act as a bar to coercive power, however complete the theory of its supremacy may be.

Thus there are limits to the state's exercise of authority, and the fact that there are suggests that in practice there seems no reason why it should not be treated as belonging to the genus of human associations. True, it is a system of order. As such it requires a body of rules to provide in their certainty and predictability a foundation for order. It needs organs to make these rules and to interpret them. Clearly it is also necessary that the state should have the use of physical force as the means of ensuring that its rules are observed. Such institutions can be accepted as a minimum, for it is apparent that states as we know them today, while they are necessarily systems of order, do not have their functions or purposes exhausted by this definition. Indeed that may well be thought of as merely a starting point. Order is merely a prerequisite for the achievement of ends which the members of the association have in common and the realization of which the state may be an instrument for realizing. An ampler and truer view of the state, derived from an examination of what states in fact do, would show it as a co-operative organization for the promotion of the welfare of its members.

This does not mean, we must hasten to add, that the co-operation is all of it voluntary or that coercion does not play a part in securing it, sometimes a very great part. Nor does it imply that all the members contribute equally to decisions or gain equally from them. But while it does not deny the presence, even the necessary presence, of coercion, it does mean that coercion cannot for long be the only bond of union, but that a certain degree and extent of willingness to co-operate and maintain the union is an essential condition of it; for this it must reflect common interests and common beliefs about them. Even the Nazi tyranny could not have remained effective without a very general success in persuading Germans that it was identified with their welfare. In order to survive, the state must surely in some considerable measure satisfy its members that it does represent a reasonably acceptable system of co-operation because it pursues what they are able to regard as their welfare. Their welfare may of course mean very different things for different societies according as they lay special stress on, or even equate it with, such contrasting ideas of good as national glory, prevalence of the race or the faith, or world revolution. It is not necessarily equivalent, although it may be at its best, to the term 'welfare' in the concept of the welfare state.

Again, the accretion of particular traditions around any given state does not seem to remove it from the genus of associations. This is, after all, a characteristic which, like that of having enforceable rules, it shares with many other human groups. This in no way belittles the importance of the fact that a state is often a principal exponent of the traditions of a community. It has a history as a social entity which sometimes extends over many centuries. In that time it has come to express a particular culture. It has developed its own customs and ways of going about its business. It forms an important, often the most important, concentration of the mutual loyalty of the group. Through its institutions it provides a regular channel for the exercise of leadership and the influencing of opinion and belief. In short, it is apt to acquire a mystique, accentuated by the use of symbols upon which the emotions of the group are fixed. All this, however, does not mean that it ceases to be an association identifiable at any given moment as consisting of a group formation of living human beings.

The state, it will then be safe to say, is an association which, like others, is created by events in which human decisions play a prominent part. This is made all the clearer if we consider the changes through which states go. Often they have been treated as though they were examples of an entity having a quality of permanence. But in fact this is not so. It is scarcely necessary to emphasize in the twentieth century, after two recent world wars, the impermanence of many states which in the nineteenth century appeared everlasting, or the permutations by which some states were merged or absorbed by others and many were created where none existed before. Indeed, those states which can claim an uninterrupted existence of more than a century are probably a minority. And it would be ridiculous to stress the quality of permanence at a time when in Europe itself there is evidently a deep and widespread dissatisfaction with the actual definition of state formations and a very real demand for the development of new types of combination, while in Asia and Africa recent history shows the birth of many new states, the division or combination of others, and a still unexhausted demand for the extension of this movement of change.

The state is clearly to be regarded as one of those groups of which all individuals are members and which, though they take a great variety of forms, can be regarded by the sociologist as possessing a generic similarity. 'Groups,' as Ginsberg says, 'may be considered as complexes of relations having a certain consistency and permanence, defined in institutions. These groups may be conceived as circles some of which fall within, while others cut across, each other. Thus the individual is a member of his family, his neighbourhood, his professional association, his church, his nation, his state, his linguistic or culture area. The relations in which he stands to these various groupings vary in depth and pervasiveness and his character is variously affected by them. The groupings themselves are not fixed but are subject to constant motion and transformation.'[1]

Thus it would seem that we have no need to regard the state as in any way a mysterious formation having supernatural or metaphysical characteristics. Nevertheless there is a constantly recurring tendency in political thought to treat the state as not belonging to the genus of associations or groups at all, but as something on altogether a different moral plane. The state is here conceived as society itself in a thoroughly comprehensive sense. In relation to this leviathan other associations are at best its creatures, and at worst are to be considered, in the words of Hobbes, as 'worms in the entrails of a natural man', because they complicate or interfere with the citizen's subordination to the one all-inclusive, omnicompetent unit.

In the mind of Burke or Hegel, indeed, the state is much more than an association of living men and women, and it is not to be regarded as subject to the same criteria of moral judgment as other associations or as the men who form them.

[1] Morris Ginsberg, *On the Diversity of Morals*, p. 157.

Where this leads is shown by Bosanquet who says that the state 'has no determinate function in a larger community, but is itself the supreme community; the guardian of a whole moral world, but not a factor within an organized moral world. Moral relations presuppose an organized life; but such a life is only within the state, and not in relations between the state and other communities.' It is true that Bosanquet is here referring to the state in its external relations, and that he elsewhere restricts its internal use of force to the 'hindering of hindrances' to free moral development. But, regarding the state as the 'operative criticism of institutions', he says again, 'By the state, then, we mean society as a unit, recognized as rightly exercising control over its members through absolute physical power'. And the significant point is that the assumption of moral rightness in its control is thus made exclusively of the state. Similar validity cannot belong to the authority exerted by other human associations over their members. This means that a church or trade union, a club or professional body, an international organization or local society can claim no like sanctity for its decisions.

Were such a proposition to be acceptable it would solve, of course, the central problem of politics, for it would establish the claim of a single authority to obedience and remove any need for further questions. To examine it makes it necessary first to remove one ambiguity in this conception itself which has been frequently the cause of confusion. Is the state here spoken of the state as it is, that is such a political entity as Great Britain or the United States? Or is it an abstract idea: the state as it ought to be? Only in the former case does this proposition solve anything. By asserting the moral supremacy of the state it predicates essential rightness—or the nearest possible approximation to it—to the law, to all decisions made by due constitutional process, and establishes the obligation to obey. If on the other hand it is an idealized state that is being spoken of, the question remains whether any such actual state conforms to it, and its claim to exercise rightful authority has to be submitted to other criteria, criteria in fact that must still lie in the disputed moral judgment of those who observe its operations. Thus the right of the state of Great Britain or the United States to demand obedience to decisions arrived at through proper legal processes will depend not on the source from which they come, as this proposition would have it, but upon a judgment as to their content, and we are no further towards solving the problem of what tests to apply in order to make that judgment a valid one. Indeed this second interpretation of what is meant by the proposition is so lacking in any useful meaning that it would be foolish to suppose that it was ever intended, were it not for the fact that those who put it forward are apt when confronted by an obviously wrong decision of an actual state to take refuge in just this interpretation. The blunt truth is that either this proposition means that the ideal state, for practical purposes at least, is the actual state or it means nothing of any practical value.

There are, it is true, refinements to this argument to which it will be necessary to return later. There is more especially the alternative assertion that while the actual state may indeed not be always perfect and may do wrong things and impose wrong decisions, either it is so much more likely to be right than any individual or group of critics within it that for all practical purposes it can be safely regarded as 'rightly exercising control over its members through absolute physical power', or since so great will be the loss from disobedience no right to disobey can be admitted.

The assertion that special sanctity attaches to the state was first based on theology and it has always kept traces of its origin. Whether medieval politics was a branch of religion or religion a branch of politics, both assumed a providential ordering of the universe, and were closely linked by this initial act of faith. Whatever sophisticating or rationalizing process is applied by later metaphysical theory there is never really absent from it this mystical first step, even though it may be scarcely explicit. Historically the feudal doctrine that the Emperor holds the world from God, just as princes hold their domains from the Emperor, fades, with the waning importance of the Empire and the growing power of princes, merging itself in the competing theory of the divine right of Kings; this, in turn, challenged by the principle *vox populi vox dei*, becomes the divine ordinance of the democratic state. All authority must come from above as long as the belief remains the same, that man is born into an ordered universe of which he is not the creator but in which he is the creature of its settled order, an order which includes established secular authority. Just as he is subject to the law of gravity so is he subject to the social order which he finds about him. He is the author of neither but both are aspects of a system, vast and infinite where he is minute and limited, over which he has no control but which is the expression of a single providential ordering of all things, a logical idea in a supreme mind. Authority is of God, an embodiment of His wisdom, the exponent and guardian of the moral world. There is a fundamental similarity between such a concept in its primitive absolutist form, where there is belief in a direct conferring of power upon the ruler as the Lord's anointed, in its later mechanical form where a machine-like universe is governed by natural law and the Almighty has retreated into constitutional monarchy, and in those more 'scientific' forms which, under the influence of the wider study of history and the discovery of evolution, depict the process of a gradual unfolding of a metaphysical Idea or Supreme Consciousness in the actual order. In all alike the sanctity of the state derives not from an evaluation of what it does but from an assertion about its nature. For each this is so closely identified with the fountainhead of authority, the creator of the universe all wise and all powerful or with an emergent Supreme Being, coming into realization through an historical process, that final sanctity attaches to the state. The order it represents is not made, nor is it to be remade by man. 'The recognition of the empirical as the ideal' follows logically from T. H. Green's perception of the universe as 'a system in which every element, being correlative to every other, at once presupposes and is presupposed by every other'. And it is a small step from asserting that our thoughts, reasoning and intelligence are real only in so far as they express a central consciousness or 'spiritual self-conscious being', to identifying the latter with the collective will incarnate in established authority.

Closely associated with this theological and metaphysical foundation of the state is what might be called the romantic theory. According to this the supreme authority of the state derives from the fact that it embodies something called the general or real will. For Kant it personifies 'the universal united will of the people' and this will 'emanates from the *a priori* Reason'. It is both a summing up of all wills when directed to the common good and an expression of a rational essence which, while contained in everyone, is enduring where they are transient. This aspect of permanence corresponds to Burke's vision of the state as 'a partnership not only between those who are living, but between those who are living, those who are dead and those who are to be born'. The common good is thus extended to include more than a momentary interest; it has its roots in tradition and its branches stretch forward into the future. Since the general will is directed to it, it determines the nature of the general will which must therefore be a determinate fact. Moreover, the common good being a moral imperative the general will corresponds to the real will of each when he wills morally. Or to put it another way—with Bosanquet: 'to obtain a full statement of what we will, what we want at any moment must at least be corrected and amended by what we want at all other moments; and this cannot be done without also correcting and amending it so as to harmonize it with what others want, which involves an application of the same process to them. But when any considerable degree of such correction and amendment had been gone through, our own will would return to us in a shape in which we should not know it again, although every detail would be a necessary inference from the whole of wishes and resolutions which we actually cherish.' The will which thus returns to us is at one and the same time our own real will and the general will. But more, it is embodied in that hierarchical complex of institutions of which the principal part is the state. To quote Bosanquet again: this 'complex of institutions is very much more complete (although imperfect) than the explicit ideas which at any given instant move any individual mind in volition'.

But there is a difficulty about both these theories. In the case of the first it must mean either that obedience is due to whatever authority was originally established at some unspecified time in the past and that no subsequent change is admissible, which is absurd, or that change can take place in the character of constituted authority without diminishing its right to claim obedience. This may mean any change which in fact occurs: *de facto* authority is *de jure* authority. Providence ordains the rule of George III until the Declaration of Independence has been successfully asserted, when it ordains the American

THE STATE: DEFINITIONS

Republic; or the Tsar one day and Lenin the next. Provided the ruler can obtain obedience, obedience is due to him. It is indeed difficult to see how any such theory can avoid the conclusion, at which Hegel arrives, that might is right.

If it means that only certain changes have this effect, how does it help in deciding which these are? If knowledge comes only in retrospect then it is still the pure determinist view. When it is alleged that only changes conforming with some particular conception of history are expressions of the ordained order of development then this historicism is still determinist for it still proclaims the sanctity of laws—this time of historical evolution—laid down for men to obey. Theirs not to exercise judgment, rational or moral, but to obey an ordained order of development. Such rules are not guides to conduct. They are predictions about conduct. They may be true or false predictions but they are irrelevant to the justification of conduct. They merely convert the sanctity of the state regarded as a static unchanging authority into the sanctity of a predetermined change in state authority. The procedure they adopt is entirely alien from, and must not be mistaken for, one which treats history as experience from which inferences can be reasonably drawn as to the desirable and the possible and which can help by providing empirical evidence for human ideals and the methods of realizing them. They do not treat history as made by men at all but as the working out of an idea in a superhuman mind, which by definition is beyond the scope of human judgment and which cannot therefore help men to know when revolt in order to change the state replaces obedience to the state as it is as the moral imperative. What seems at first to be implied by the theory is that it never does. Revolution cannot be justified—in advance. But since revolutions do in fact take place the hypothesis does not fit the facts and so must be discarded. Only if it be admitted instead, as the more sophisticated form of the theory accepted, that providence may work through the revolutionary as well as the established order can the theory be regarded as consistent with itself. But in that case it helps in no way to show when the revolutionary rather than the established ruler is the true agent of providence. All it seems to make in effect is the unhelpful assertion that there is a moral obligation to obey only when there is no practical alternative.

In the second case also there is no answer to the essential questions about the basis of political obligation. It is obviously true that a man's will is at some times based on a better judgment than at others. His momentary inclination will conflict with the fulfilment of another desire. His 'trivial' will may be incompatible with his more enduring will. It may be based on incomplete awareness of the facts. It may not take into account a social good which also he would perhaps, on more mature reflection, wish to see achieved. Indeed a logical construction of all his wishes, in which they were harmonized to create an integrated whole, might certainly appear to him as an unrecognizable will which it could be argued was his 'real will' in the sense that it was more consistent with himself over a longer period of time. It would be an amalgam of his actual wills of many moments in time. Even so it could only be said to be a different will from that of any particular moment. It would not be a comprehensive will unless it included every moment. And although it might be argued that it was more likely to be a better will than his momentary will it would at most be relatively better and at worst might be a less good will than one of those which it amalgamated. Or if this real will be taken not as an amalgam of actual but transient wills but as the result of a synthesis of ends willed, or purposes, constructed into a logically harmonious whole and so determining the single means to its achievement as the one and only possible, therefore 'real', will, this is in either case no more than to claim the possibility of making such an abstraction of an ideal will. It does not prove, or even give any good reason for supposing, that its identity can be practically discovered, still less that it is expressed in law, government or institutions. For the social good willed as an end is not an objective or determinable fact. There may be as many interpretations of it as there are individual judgments. And there is no criterion other than judgment itself by which to test the validity of varying interpretations. Thus these general will theories have either to revert to the mystical assumption of a common self or Supreme Being the Idea in whose mind is the real will of every lesser being, or they merely assert the platitude that some wills are based on more mature reflection and wider knowledge than others, and some pay more attention to the social advantage.

It is at first sight puzzling that such a view of the state should have gained the acceptance it has. And it may be wondered why something which can be described simply and empirically should attract such complicated and metaphysical explanations. But it is easier to lay down the law than to persuade, and in matters of such importance as observance of morality and the law there is a strong temptation to grasp anything which suggests that they are beyond question. Clearly it is to the advantage of those in authority that such a view should prevail. But more generally, there is always an important body of people who, because they feel their interests to be at stake, want others to obey the established system of order. Therefore there is among them—and they are likely to be the most powerful element in the society—a natural tendency to welcome a theory which seems to strengthen it. For them, too, it is naturally preferable to regard morality as an objective pattern made for man and not by man, and to encourage people to think of the laws and the moral code as established beyond question and not requiring substantiation, to think of goodness as lying in conformity with this pattern and in obedience to the state.

Such an attitude is reinforced by all the influences which hinder the belief that men can control their fate, and which induce in them resignation, complacency, and conservatism. First is fear; the tendency of this is to make them followers of Hobbes, anxious only for an authority to which they can cling for protection and upon which to shuffle off responsibility. At bottom this fear is that any admission of possible error in the established code may open the flood gates to anarchy. So we must think: 'All discord, harmony not understood, All partial evil, universal good.' Secondly, there is doubt about human nature and its capacity for decency or improvement. Man being naturally wicked, a victim of original sin, pessimism as to his prospects logically follows—unless the strongest defence-works are erected against his natural tendencies. And what can offer stronger defence-works than supernatural forces beyond the categories of time and space, doctrines of grace and revelation, and ordained rule. Thirdly is scepticism, that distrust of reason which is an invitation to seek for a firmer foundation for order in truths that transcend reason and can only be perceived by mystical processes. This is the appeal to a 'higher reason' of heart and conscience, which has been made by many since Pascal. Coleridge, for example, appropriated the term to a use which was really its converse and, substituting 'understanding' for reason, could be claimed by Carlyle to have discovered 'the sublime secret of believing by the reason what the understanding had been obliged to fling out as incredible'. Discovery of the 'imperfections of natural reason' may lead people, as Hume recognized, to 'fly to revealed truth with the greatest avidity'.

Interested teaching discourages, not always with any clear consciousness of doing so, the consideration of facts inconvenient to those established in power. There is evidence also to suggest, as for instance that given by Professor Popper in his argument on the motivation of Hegel, that there may sometimes be deliberate intention to serve authority behind a particular political theory. Clearly scientific beliefs must cover the facts up to a certain point necessary for dealing with them in everyday life. The assumption that the world is flat, for instance, or that it is composed of mind and matter, may satisfy nearly all the needs of daily existence. There is a danger, however, in the very facility with which a hypothesis such as this is found to work. It is only too tempting to regard the margins where it does not work as providing exceptions which at most modify but which do not invalidate its essential truth, whereas it is in fact at this point only that its essential falsity becomes apparent. Such is no less true in the field of political than in that of physical speculation. The idealist theory of the state commends itself to those who, whether because they are concerned with the enforcement of law and order or because it is to their advantage to support established institutions, seek a philosophical justification of the powers that be.

Then again, when we compare the individual with the state, he seems so small and transient and it so vast and enduring that it is tempting to regard him as, if not its creature, at least irrelevant to its proceedings and irresponsible for them. He cannot on his own deflect it from its course. Is not his place then simply to acquiesce, accept all that it does as he accepts the weather or the movement of the earth? Is it not best for him to cultivate resignation to the forces of history which determine its operations since he cannot hope to control them, and to look with the detachment of the sceptic on the self-important gyrations of those who persuade themselves that by entering the conflict they are influencing events? Such an attitude to practical problems corresponds naturally with an organic theory of the state, which considers it as a natural growth from the life and character of a people, and not as something which can be shaped by the people themselves according to their own will and purpose.

It is surely no accident that the organic theory should have flourished in a country like nineteenth century Germany unaccustomed to self-government and used to the hand of a strong executive, and that it should never have been put forward in quite so uncompromising a form in a country like England with its long experience of limited government. Such a view, too, seems to be often accepted just when men have most clearly shown that they can, and do in fact, take their political institutions in hand and direct them or remould them according to their will, as in the French reaction to the Revolution, or in America after the Civil War. For then it comes in response to disorder or, as in the case of Germany after Napoleon, to defeat and the weakness of disunity. There is perhaps a similar cause for the development of such an attitude after the experience of a great modern war. Although it is true that the first effects of such an experience are to break the bonds of habit, releasing energy, opening new vistas by experiment and inventiveness, and making men aware of the great possibilities of collective achievement, nevertheless war unleashes such vast forces and makes apparent how difficult they are to control, that it is apt to give man individually a sense of insignificance beside them, and to encourage an attitude of fatalistic irresponsibility in regard to them. It may be the case also that the very necessity for strong authority and leadership in wartime may diminish the habit of self-reliance in matters of collective concern. And the direct experience of the perils of international anarchy may clothe organic theories of the state with the comforts of order and security, and create in them an island of certainty in an ocean of doubt.

Now all such theories of the state assume, of necessity, that a fundamental uniqueness attaches to it, at least in relation to morality. But if, as we have been arguing, it is to be regarded as belonging to the genus of associations or groups, then we should expect to find that similar claims to exclusive moral authority are made for other associations. This, indeed, is in fact just what we do find; and the possibility that such claims can be urged should surely put us on our guard against accepting any such assumption of uniqueness. Figgis, for instance, spoke of the 'corporate personality' of societies other than the state, asserting that 'this unity of life and action is a thing which grows up naturally and inevitably in bodies of men united for a permanent end', and that 'this real life and personality' is something which 'they possess by the nature of the case and not by the arbitrary grant of the sovereign'. What he claimed primarily, though not exclusively, for a church has of course been asserted by many others before and since in the long struggle between church and state. Again, syndicalists and group socialists have made similar claims in more recent times for the trade union. The vocational association, either because it represents a vital social function, or because of the intimacy of its concern with the day-to-day activities of its members, a concern which has seemed to syndicalists both more comprehensive and less remote than that of the state, may appear to enjoy a moral authority of a specially fundamental kind. Or again, in the closely knit world of today, there are not wanting those who are willing to assert the superior claims upon human loyalty of group formations like federal unions or international organizations that extend beyond the boundaries of the state and include several states within them. It must surely be clear that in the competition between such different types of association there is no self-evident or *a priori* basis for the claims of the state. In order finally to dispose of them it may be worthwhile to give a last glance at the arguments supporting the assumption on which organic theories are founded.

The first is that the state is the 'natural' expression of the community. Men are indeed usually born members of a state. They exercise no choice in the matter, and grow up under its inherited compulsions, with no one to ask whether they wish to belong to it, and with big, though not unsuperable difficulties in the way of leaving it. But then surely the state is not unique in these characteristics. A man belongs naturally to a family, and anthropology suggests similar natural tendencies to membership of a clan or tribe. Nor have there been lacking those who have asserted a like 'natural' membership of a church or the superiority of his membership of the human race over his qualities as the citizen of any smaller unit however powerfully organized or however much patriotism is strengthened by the bonds of kinship, language, or tradition. All that we can say is that it is 'natural' to men to form groups and associations, and that this quality of 'naturalness' cannot be shown to attach specially to any one type. Moreover, there is always movement both of persons from one to another association, and in the forms which such associations take.

This brings us to the second possible basis for singularity, that which we have already discussed under the heading of force or compulsion. But nothing is clearer in the modern world than the fact of continual movement of persons out of the state. Not only is this a process of individual migration, but it may be one of the departure of a group, like the large number of loyalists who migrated during and after the American revolutionary war. The tragic existence of hordes of refugees bears witness today to the incompleteness which any claims to exercise compulsion have in defining the character of the state. The fact surely is that while elements of compulsion enter into many associations, such, for instance, as a church, a party, or a trade union, they do not differ, except perhaps in degree, in the state when this is compared with other group formations. If the ties of work, language, property, social connection, habit and tradition, as well as economic cost and risk and fear of the unknown, create for most people too great an obstacle to voluntary expatriation, the fact still remains that they can and do leave the state. And although only one in a thousand normally migrates in any one year from such a country as Great Britain, the principle is not affected by the quantity: men may and do contract out of the state. While it must be admitted, of course, that, while a man may leave one state, he cannot leave all states, but can only leave one at the cost of joining another, this does not affect the issue, for we are concerned, not with all states taken together as a unit, but with any state as a unit, and a man's relation to it is thus shown to be in some measure voluntary.

Finally, there is the claim that the state has a more important function than other associations. But that imports into the consideration a judgment of ends: what function is more important than another is a matter of opinion. The citizen who defies the state because he feels a keener loyalty to his church, or his fellow workers, or his race, or his principles of humanity, is denying the priority claimed by the state, and who is to judge between him and it? Any such claim to supremacy on the part of the state derives from a judgment that the ends it serves have a universal priority. But the priority of these ends, whether they be—with Hobbes—to maintain order, or—with Bentham—to secure happiness, is by no means self-evident. There are many kinds of order, the order of a concentration camp or of a society of co-operating equals. And even the happiness of the greatest number may be interpreted in different ways, as of differently constituted majorities having different ideas of what makes for happiness. There is no *a priori* pre-eminence in the end itself. The ends served by any particular state have not a universal priority because in fact we often prefer other, conflicting, ends. States vary profoundly in character. It is impossible to claim that the one into which a man happens to be born has a pre-emptive claim upon him. Besides, states change in constitution from time to time; they also change in their territorial basis. Overnight two states become one, as with England and Scotland, or one state becomes two as has happened in the low countries, in Scandinavia and elsewhere. What metaphysical change corresponds to this physical metamorphosis? What permutations occurred in the real will or the common self of the people of Alsace-Lorraine to justify either their expression by Berlin from 1870 or by Paris from 1918? Surely the implication that something of this kind took place in them is too much to accept in either case, and the whole theory falls to the ground if only for that reason. There is too the fact, which makes this point of special practical importance today, that probably never since the development of the modern nation state in the last four centuries have so many people, especially in western Europe, more seriously doubted the adequacy of the political entities to which they belong. They are aware both of inherent incapacities in these for meeting their needs for such things as security and economic order, and, increasingly, of the possibilities in alternative, particularly federal, forms. Since, therefore, we can say not only that individuals can opt, but that large groups and even whole communities are showing signs of actually opting, for different forms of state, it seems especially important that we should recognize the provisional nature of these.

If, then, it seems unsuitable to regard the state, either by reason of what it is or of what it does, as *sui generis*, it re-enters the company of other associations. The questions it is worth while asking about them are proper to be asked about it also. If it is not the creature or expression of a transcendent force, we must treat it, just as we do other associations, as the creature of its actual members. If it does not express a superhuman will or purpose it must be considered as expressing the will or purpose of the human beings within it. 'Its fundamental law is not a code or law of nature, but,' as Lindsay wrote, 'a constitution or machinery, an agreed way of settling differences.' Thus the important facts about it are the nature of the agreement of its members that it represents, and the way in which it serves their purposes, as is the case with other associations. And what is needed is an analysis of its character in just these terms. Its value, that is to say, is always a relative value, relative to its members, to be found in their judgment and their evaluation of its acts, and not in any of those simple absolutes which political theorists once sought. Its members will find it good in so far as they recognize in its performance the achievement of ends they deem good. The first step is, therefore, to consider what can usefully be said about what these ends are.

For what this amounts to is that since the state cannot be derived from abstract principles about the nature of the universe, such as metaphysical formulas, laws of historical development, or scientific hypotheses of biological evolution, it is not in them that relevant criteria are to be found. Regarding it as an association among many, however special its characteristics, we shall be less tempted to seek for such dogmas. Because, instead, we treat it as a system of co-operation among men to achieve their purposes—or, more humbly, to get what they want out of life—we shall look for the standards to apply in an examination of what are men's current purposes, or what they actually want out of life. But this is not to say that we cannot make useful generalizations about these. Nor is it to refuse to recognize that many are in fact influenced by their own hypotheses of a metaphysical, biological, historical or other character in building up their purposes or in developing their ideas of what they want.

FOUNDATIONS AND CRITERIA

'POLITICAL ideals will vary according to men's views on human destiny,' said Saint Thomas Aquinas. 'Those who are persuaded that the purpose of life is pleasure, or power, or honour, will reckon that state best arranged in which they can live comfortably, or acquire great wealth, or achieve great power and lord it over many. Others who think that the crowning good of virtue is the purpose of our present life will want an arrangement under which men can live virtuously and peaceably together. In short, political judgment will be settled by the sort of life a man expects and proposes to lead by living in community.'

This is to suggest that we shall expect to find the purpose of political society in the purposes of its members and nowhere else. In this it is like all other associations; what distinguishes it primarily from them is the purpose it represents. Political theory must start, therefore, by considering what can be said about the character of human purposes.

Since different purposes require different means for their fulfilment, there is a secondary feature which distinguishes one association from another. This is its characteristic organization, which means both the regulations ordering relationships within it and the instruments and powers with which it is provided as necessary for pursuing its ends. These are the corollary of its purpose; its purpose is not the corollary of the powers and instruments with which it is endowed. The state has the use of force to achieve its ends; its ends do not result from its possession of force.

Thus a church exists to promote a doctrine and perhaps a way of life and acts of worship. It makes rules for its members, has its own governing authorities, constitution, and buildings where its group life can be carried on. The reason for its existence is a particular purpose which a group holds in common. Nor need there be anything narrow or static in that purpose. The insistence by Figgis that an association is not a creation of the state, nor bound by its original document, but that it has a life of its own—to repeat the quotation of him: 'this unity of life and action which grows up naturally and inevitably in bodies of men united for a permanent end'—corresponds to an essential fact about associations. They are dynamic in the sense that the purpose for which they exist, on which their members are united, is dynamic; its content is not defined once for all in an original constitution drawn up by the dead, but is constantly being redefined by the living. Common purpose as it has meaning for the group makes the association, whether it be church, trade union, alliance of states, or parish club. While it exists the association has meaning; when it disappears the association tends to dissolve.

In most cases there is little difficulty in deciding what are the purposes for which an association exists. We ask how its members define them. And we can do the same thing of the state. Put in another way we may ask what its members expect of it. Since the state is a structure with a long history of speculation attached to it we may well find that it is useful at certain points to consider what thinkers in the past on this subject have had to say about its purpose.

Now this is essentially to say that our enquiry must be grounded in human nature. Some modern political theorists object to this proposition because they think that human nature is so complex and various that any generalization about it must, if true, be too vague to have any useful meaning. Thus J. C. Rees writes that 'whatever principle we choose, it is not likely to cover all cases, and if we try to provide for the exceptions by making it more general and vague it loses its usefulness'; that 'the search for a general answer to questions about the purpose of the state, for an all-embracing principle that determines our political obligation . . . seems to be quite unprofitable'; and that 'insofar as political philosophy attempts to deduce certain practical precepts from theories of the universe or dogmas about the ultimate nature of matter or even axioms relating to man's intrinsic nature, the critics have an unanswerable case, because political institutions and political programmes are just not derivable from such abstract formulas'.[1]

Much of all this is perfectly true, as we have already seen when considering attempts to treat the state as having its essence determined by some theory of the universe. But the criticism goes too far when it denies the possibility of finding any foundations for political theory of any kind. For if we treat the state as an association we shall see that its purpose must be grounded in the needs of its members and must somehow translate their purposes as these needs produce them. Thus the consideration of human nature, that is of men's needs, desires, ideas, will necessarily enter into the discussion, and it is difficult to see how anything else can usefully do so. It is perfectly true that we do not need to assume, because this is the case, that the result must be the discovery of some simple axiom or that everything can be summed up in one simple assertion about the purpose of the state which will be comprehensive, of universal applicability, and at the same time useful for providing clear answers to all practical political problems.

Nor on the other hand do we need to conclude, as seems to be the tendency of modern critics of political theory who have been influenced by G. E. Moore and the so-called revolution in philosophy, that every attempt at providing foundations for political theory from Plato and Aristotle to Green, Hobhouse, and Laski is logically valueless. It is contended that the answers given to general questions such as Why should we obey the state? or Why is democracy better than dictatorship? or Why was it wicked to send people to Belsen? or How can liberty be reconciled with authority? are tautologies; nothing can be deduced from them. They are improper questions or unnecessary ones which can only be posed from a mistaken notion of the nature of reasoning in this sort of subject.

The argument that no foundations can be discovered by political theory, that there are no 'fundamental rules from which others can be deduced', as Weldon puts it,[2] is both true and false; or at least it can be used in a misleading way to

[1] 'The Limitations of Political Theory', in *Political Studies*, Vol. II, No. 3, p. 253.
[2] T. D. Weldon, *The Vocabulary of Politics*, p. 97.

suggest that they are necessarily meaningless or valueless. True enough that they are not to be treated as axioms, demonstrable, susceptible of proof, or self-evident, and that they have often been treated as though they were. True too that this arises from a misunderstanding of what is the character of statements of this type and of what they can do. 'It is pointless,' says Weldon, 'to invent an axiom that men ought always to be treated as ends in themselves in order to demonstrate the truth of "It was wicked to send people to Belsen or Buchenwald", for this is not the sort of statement which requires or admits of demonstration.'[1] He claims that to ask why it is wrong to torture people in concentration camps is a 'mistaken question'. And later he asserts that the only ultimate test in such matters of whether an appraisal is correct is a personal view 'or prejudice if that word is preferred'.[2]

But the fact is that people often do want to ask these 'mistaken questions', and they are not readily satisfied with an ultimate reference to mere personal prejudices. Nor has it been customary among political theorists to be satisfied. What then have they been attempting to do when they enunciated foundations or fundamental or first principles? First it is clear that they are making an appraisal of some sort. What is the special character of this kind of appraisal? Surely it is imply that they are attempting a summary. Their principle represents an effort to bring order and consistency into the process of reporting on the world of experience, and this is a process familiar in all branches of science. Such a principle, it is true, is not amenable to proof or demonstration in the manner of pure science. On the contrary, it does in the last resort express no more than a point of view. But what surely makes it more than a mere personal prejudice is that it is possible to give reasons for it and that it makes sense to ask for reasons, that we expect these to be consistent with one another and with any other principles associated with this one, as well as with practical deductions from it.

Appraisals do not just happen. There are reasons for them. They connect with other value-judgments, we are open to persuasion about them and normal ways in which persuasion is

[1] T. D. Weldon, *The Vocabulary of Politics*, p. 99.
[2] *Ibid.*, p. 176.

brought to bear are by showing their logical consequences or the effects of their application in practice.

But this is by no means to say that the appraisals which the political theorist formulates as a 'foundation' or fundamental principle will furnish readymade answers to all political problems or even that they must provide precise criteria for judging any political issue. Because we do not know exactly what is the social good at a given moment or what is the best development of personality we are not precluded from saying that the social good or the development of personality is a part, or even the whole, of the purpose of the state. These may be, or they may not be, useful practical ways of summarising multifarious objectives, each of which taken separately would command support. Thus freedom of speech, of worship, of association, of choice of work, and of education have been successively asserted as proper objectives of state policy, and the notion of development of personality can be claimed to be a method, good or bad, of summarizing them, bringing out an essential common element in them, showing a certain orderly relationship in them, and, as it were, articulating an aim only half consciously implicit in any one of them. This manner of proceeding would be as legitimate, and on the whole more nearly related to the historic process of their achievement, as to assert that development of personality is the fundamental principle from which each such claim can be logically deduced. Nor need the summary statement, or the 'foundation', be regarded as useful only in its capacity to illuminate them and to bring order and consistency into their variety; it may also offer some guidance for future programmes of state activity. That some such usefulness can be claimed for it does not mean, however, that it will resolve all practical difficulties; nor should it be condemned if it cannot be shown to resolve any. To give reasons why we think it wrong to torture people in concentration camps is not valueless if it clarifies and makes more consistent and orderly our views of proper social organization and the ends we expect it to serve. There is certainly a stage at which it is pointless to ask further questions or demand more reasons, but in the process of reaching that stage we may expect to find common ground with others in making our appraisals, and this common ground is of great importance. Although we cannot prove the validity of the final result we may be able to evoke widespread agreement and, by showing empirically the probable practical consequences of contrary principles, we may make disagreement more difficult or, at least, more aware of what it involves.

We might supplement, for instance, the argument that it is wrong to torture people in concentration camps. We could say that we should regard it as an evil were it applied to ourselves, and that a principle of reciprocal treatment is relevant here. We might say that such treatment is wrong because it satisfies no need of which we are aware but on the contrary causes needless pain. We could say too that it obviously prevents the free development of personality and individual happiness. And we could continue that since we want these things for ourselves we must want them for others if we are to expect their co-operation in social arrangements. In saying that we want security from this sort of thing or that life would be intolerable were it practised we may be merely stating a preference, it is true, but it may surely be said that the combination of such statements serves in some measure to elucidate and make more coherent the principle and its application.

How does such an approach to 'foundations' relate to the view that ' . . . the political theorist will not have to invent criteria for appraising the behaviour of officials and politicians or assessing the merits of party programmes. These are already to hand in the society around him'?[1] Now it is true that there are many such criteria 'constantly being applied and we rarely think to question them . . . security of person and property, orderliness and predictability in human relations, satisfaction of basic material needs, promotion of artistic appreciation, and so on. . . . These standards are available to us as part of the way of life into which we gradually learn to fit ourselves with differing degrees of protest and success. We do not depend on philosophies for their existence, though some philosophies have contributed to their popularity. We are therefore equipped for the business of appraisal without having to rely on the formulas laid down by political theorists; that is to say, we need make no assumptions about the state having a single purpose to fulfil, or there being just one ground of political obligation,

[1] J. C. Rees, *op. cit.*, p. 256, and as elaborated in a paper delivered to the political studies conference 1955.

as a condition of employing these criteria effectively.'

While there is much truth in all this, it must surely be qualified in several ways. First, there is not 'an agreed set of criteria', as Rees himself says, and 'we sometimes apply different standards and from them support conflicting policies'. Certainly a citizen of Nazi Germany or Communist Russia would not accept some of them and would attach quite different meanings to others than we do. Secondly, the criteria are not necessarily consistent with one another. Rees again himself gives the example of conflict between the criteria of 'one's fellows', 'the community', and 'the modern world'. Thirdly, no immutability belongs to many of 'the criteria to hand in the society about us'. Those by which we should judge the behaviour of officials or politicians are not the same in the eighteenth and the twentieth century. In another country or a different period bribery evokes no moral condemnation, and the purchase of preferment is an accepted principle of public administration. Fourthly, we do in fact find, as might be expected from such divergencies as these, that we sometimes want to ask for reasons for such criteria, to discover on what they are based. And so finally it may surely be claimed that, there being nothing final in 'the criteria to hand', we may need to explain why we use them, to choose between them, to improve them, to justify them by appealing to other, possibly more profound or comprehensive, ideas of purpose. In short, we may wish to clarify them by relating them to one another in a conceptual unity. Indeed it is difficult to see how otherwise we can embark on the process of justification or improvement which the above qualifications imply as necessary. As to this process there is no difficulty in accepting Rees's own admirable summary: 'As Hume showed, there is no way of proving, demonstratively, that one particular set of values is superior to another, but it may be that, in Mill's words, "considerations may be presented capable of determining the intellect either to give or to withhold its assent". Too often do we assume, under the influence of fashionable gibes at the "intellectual fallacy", that moral disagreements cannot be resolved in principle by further enquiry into the criteria and facts adduced by each side.' So perhaps there is no difference of opinion here, after all!

It is perhaps the case that much of this dislike of the attempt to find formulas is attributable to an undue fear of stating the obvious. But it is after all to be expected that in seeking to make general statements of any kind about what is commonly accepted, or what is common purpose, we shall have to make commonplace statements. We are liable to go wrong if we are afraid of saying what we do not ordinarily want to say only because everyone knows it to be so and is consequently prone to find tiresome the statement of it. For the commonplace may express an insight which it is important to bear in mind; and to avoid stating it in deference to good manners may lead us to fail to make use of it, or even to suppose that there is something suspect or misleading in it. This point has been interestingly made by A. N. Prior in a talk of 'The Revolution in Philosophy',[1] when he said that he was sure that no solution of such problems was to be found by 'casting out automatically what people do not ordinarily say or want to say. . . . If we are not allowed to find our own ways of recording insights which people either do not ordinarily have or do not ordinarily think worth mentioning, then philosophy is being made the instrument of a colossal tyranny of the commonplace and the conventional. . . . There are a great many questions,' he continues, 'which we do not commonly hear being asked simply because everybody knows the answer to them, and unless you happen to be setting an examination it is generally a piece of impertinence to ask somebody something which you already know, and he knows you know, and you knows he knows, and he knows you know he knows. If we are going to study ordinary usage let us study it properly and recognize that a great deal of ordinary usage is simply a matter of social etiquette, with no further significance whatever.' It is surely important that we should not allow common assumptions to be given less weight than they deserve for fear that by stating them we shall offend against good manners because we shall appear to throw doubt upon the commonsense of those with whom we are entering into discussion.

Thus we are not postulating some such axiom as that freedom or happiness, the fulfilment of personality or self-realization is the greatest good and that this is either self-evident, a part of natural law, or a super-empirical reality.

[1] On the BBC Third Programme, January 22, 1957.

FOUNDATIONS AND CRITERIA

But we are examining the process by which appraisals or empirical judgments are made by individuals, and making inductive generalizations about it. First it is an intelligent or rational process. That is not to say that there is one right answer as when we say that 2+2 are 4, or that this corresponds to Objective Reason or to the judgment of the Great Appraiser of us all. But it is to say that we can give reasons. Examples are: 'I like his generosity but I think he carries it to the point of encouraging idleness in others'; 'The Health Service is good because it ensures treatment but it leads to some waste of drugs'; 'It is important not to leave litter on a beauty spot'.

Secondly it involves likes and dislikes and thus expresses personal preferences. In these examples, for generosity, medical treatment, 'unspoilt' natural scenery, and against idleness, waste, untidiness. So that there may be disagreement from those who prefer parsimony to charity, prayer to medicine, or who think well of inactivity and ill of those who spend time and energy on orderliness. And while there may be reasonable argument on the merits of such alternatives there is no necessary agreement that one is right nor can there be any proof that another is wrong.

If one basis for regularity is to be found in the rational element the second element, of preference, cannot be regarded, for all its evident uncertainties, as the result of the pure play of chance. On the contrary there is plenty of room for the discovery of regularities within this realm of apparent free choice. It may be suggested that on the whole the individual in making his appraisals will be guided by the wish to satisfy felt needs. When Mr Weldon proposes as one of his 'not final or conclusive tests' for preferring one political system to another the question 'does it censor the reading of those who are subject to it and impose restrictions on teaching?' this, we suspect, is closely connected with satisfying certain needs of mental activity. Another test 'does it secure a living wage?' would be intimately concerned with the need for bodily survival.

But this suggests that the search here for regularities is leading us back into an examination of human nature and its needs and that we are seeking for common elements within it or common demands made by the members of a community for what they regard as satisfactions. These of course will show some tendency to vary according to conditions as well as to be held in common. One group may set greater store by the pleasures of leisure and contemplation even at the cost of having fewer means of material satisfaction; another may regard these latter as more important even if the cost is a degree of activity leaving little over for leisure or contemplation. But both are concerned with the pleasure gained from the satisfaction of felt needs. And it is surely also true that views of the character of needs and of the qualities of satisfaction will be often affected by, and will affect, beliefs on much wider questions, such as those which are asked in history, biology, theology, physics, philosophy. Tawney's *Religion and the Rise of Capitalism* shows just such a relationship between a Protestant cosmology and both the needs felt and the satisfactions valued in a particular kind of acquisitive society. Herbert Spencer's *Social Statics* is itself the expression of an interlocking interpretation of history, through a doctrine of biological evolution, and of needs and satisfactions in society. If we want to understand the culture and behaviour of a primitive community it is not irrelevant to know that it believes in a jealous god and derives satisfaction from appeasing him through such activities as fasting, building temples, human sacrifice, or attacking a particular enemy; though we may of course understand even better if we can see reasons why they might want to attack that particular enemy anyway. 'The Canaanites and the Aztecs saw some of the cosmic powers as beings who were malevolent but not fully competent without human aid, so that they would be likely to cut off mankind's light and water if they were not appeased and fortified with human sacrifices. For us, the Canaanite-Aztec picture is revolting, as well as unconvincing, though, for the people who saw the cosmos like that, human sacrifice was obligatory.'[1]

This is in fact the sort of approach we make in attempting to understand any group of people. We apply it in studying, say, the Conservative Party or the Communist movement. It is the regularity in appraisals which makes sense of it and distinguishes it from the other. Each is constituted by a set of beliefs and reasonings, and of preferences and attitudes. Psychologists like Professor Eysenk may even deem it worthwhile to attempt

[1] Professor Toynbee in *The Observer*, March 6, 1955.

to establish statistical correlations between them. The analyst of political theories and the historian of political thought and the social philosopher describe and explain them from their own respective angles.

The party, as an institution coming into being with the special purpose of determining the action of the state, has a distinctively political end and can also be looked at from the point of view of its effect in and on the bigger community of which it is a part and whose ideas and behaviour it is endeavouring to assimilate to its own beliefs and preferences. But this only gives it a double significance for political studies. In its first aspect, looked at as it were from within, it is naturally approached as we would any other group, such as a social class, or an association like a church, by assessing its system of appraisals or *weltanschauung*, its valuation of needs and satisfactions, and the behaviour with which these accord.

Now it would certainly seem that it is just such matters as these that are being considered in the classical English tradition of political theory. Here it may be said are its foundations because it is on any regularities they reveal that politics can be built—whether it be in terms of happiness with the utilitarians and Mill, of self-realization with Green, Hobhouse, and Laski, or of basic needs with Ginsberg. But sometimes—and most clearly with Green—we are certainly faced with the attempt to fit the axiom into a system of super-empirical reality, to give it a metaphysical essence, and to draw deductive conclusions from it. Here however we are deriving our foundations inductively from what in fact individuals do in making empirical judgments.

We are suggesting first that there is something common in the process: it is a matter of intelligence (or reason) and preference and represents a plan for conduct which is thus approved; what it issues in may be called, according to taste, self-realization or happiness or the satisfaction of needs.

Secondly, it provides a 'foundation' for democratic politics inasmuch as it finds the basis of community in regularities or agreement within the field of appraisals, preferences, or beliefs.

III

PURPOSE

(a) *The Good Life*

SO when we turn to consider what can usefully be said about the purpose of the state we are not seeking any single self-evident axiom from which all else can be derived or an all-embracing principle that determines our political obligation. Nor are we reading into the question the assumption that an answer must exist in the form of a comprehensive phrase applicable to all states at all times and solving all practical issues. But we are seeking for regularity and coherence in ideas on the subject. And we can make that search by examining what is commonly thought and more particularly what are the specific ideas about the ends of the state propounded by political philosophers. The process cannot be exhaustive, of course, and, being selective, must be regarded as partial, tentative, and incomplete.

It will take us first into a realm where psychology, biology, or any knowledge of the make-up and working of the human being may be expected to throw light; here it is primarily a study of man isolated, for the purposes of that study, from his environment. The second angle of approach will be rather social and environmental and here it is knowledge of the institutions and rules in which ideas are embodied, or through which needs are met, which may be expected to forward the enquiry we are undertaking.

Aristotle thought of the state as existing to promote the good life of its citizens. Such an idea is clearly general and vague enough to invite those who regard as unprofitable the search for principles of political theory to say of it 'that it may mean anything or nothing'. Whether it can be given sufficient precision and elucidation to meet this criticism can be examined in due course. Since it appears, however, to have been a common assumption of much political speculation since Aristotle, it may serve at least to start from.

One point that it brings out is certainly not without value; that is not only the close connection between morals and politics, but the reason why, as Hobhouse said, we should consider that in this sense 'politics must be subordinate to ethics'.[1] As Bertrand de Jouvenel remarks, politics is to be thought of as a moral, rather than a social, science because it is concerned with the problem of ethical harmony, or agreement between the individual and his fellows as to what he should and should not do.[2] While this point of view is correct in asserting the moral basis of politics, on the other hand, since the study of morality itself involves the study of society, we shall not find the opposition it implies between morality and the social sciences is a helpful one. Politics, like morality, requires attention to both. When Ginsberg makes one of his tests of moral development 'the growth of insight into the nature and conditions of well-being made possible by wider experience of human needs and capacities and of the conditions of social co-operation,'[3] he is in fact indicating the twin facets of the consideration necessary for our study. The first, 'human needs and capacities', belongs most immediately to an examination of the concept of the good life, and has primary moral implications; the second, 'the conditions of social co-operation', while it has these also, stresses rather the need for the study of social institutions and organization.

From such a preliminary analysis certain assumptions implicit in our approach become apparent. The first is that we are not regarding the state as an end in itself but as a means to something sought by its members. It may be taken secondly that such an end is not to be thought of as an absolute capable of interpretation in some form which is self-evident or unchanging. On the contrary what is regarded as the good life is likely to change with changing views of human needs and of the

[1] *Elements of Social Justice*, 1930, p. 13.
[2] See his 'A Discussion of Freedom' in *The Cambridge Journal*, Vol. VI, No. 12, September 1953.
[3] *Diversity of Morals*, pp. 119–20.

possibilities of satisfying them. But it follows too that the value of the state at any given moment, the use made of it, and the way it is organized must depend upon an estimate of its significance in helping its members to achieve the good life.

Again, when we make the good life a starting point for analysing its purposes we are not giving the state a prescriptive authority over other associations, many of which may also claim to serve this same end. Although they usually do so in a more specific and limited way, the state's purpose is not more, or less, important by virtue of being general, and indeed the valuation put upon its activities by comparison with those of other associations, or of the individual acting on his own, will itself be found to vary from time to time. Comparison with the church affords an obvious example. There is an idea of a totality of ends, an interlacing pattern of them, implicit in the concept of the good life, and it would seem to follow from this that any association, including the state, must be valued in relation to them, as an instrumentality for their achievement. Far from giving the state a different basis and a special claim to authority, we are thus assimilating it to other associations, and saying that all alike are to be treated as systems of social co-operation for satisfying needs.

With these preliminaries it may be possible to consider whether the concept can be given sufficient precision to make it useful. In doing so it will be best to look first at the individual, and second at the social, aspects of the question, although both are of course closely interwoven. The need to make the approach from these two angles is again made apparent, although with a slight variation, if we examine such a typical statement of social aims as these are conceived today throughout the world as we find in the UNESCO symposium on human rights. Of this Ginsberg says 'Everywhere the concern is ultimately with the liberation of personality and the equalization of conditions under which different personalities may develop. Everywhere the problem is what can be done by organized effort to assure equal freedom in a common life.'[1]

What we find in the discussion of purpose in a general way is that although the proposition may be attempted in the form of a summarizing concept, and these summaries vary, there is

[1] *Diversity of Morals*, page 114.

nevertheless a clearly apparent association between them. They have common elements and differences of emphasis. Both what is common and what is different may serve to clarify our thought on the subject. There is a patent connection between such enunciated principles of objective as the good life, virtue, self-realization, fulfilment of personality, beatitude, happiness, and even maximization of pleasure.

As we enter upon the process of attempting to bring these together in relation to the individual human being, it is clear that there is first a conditioning element outside his control. As a physical being he is subject to a set of circumstances of a physical order. These hem him in and restrict his freedom. He has certain rudimentary wants which must be met if he is to reach a minimum of contentment; and the manner and degree of meeting them will affect the degree of his fulfilment and happiness. Basic needs exist in him for food, clothing, shelter. Health is a conditioning factor too. He is beset by scarcities, uncertainties and dangers and the knowledge of death; and the fear of these must always in some measure be with him. Something he can do on his own to increase his security from them, and much by co-operation with others, but the limitations are severe and there is always a point where they are beyond his control.

While, however, the needs and the limitations are there as a conditioning element, the ways in which they are felt, their impact on him have immense variety. Different men want different kinds of food, clothes and shelter and security. They also want freedom to choose their different kinds, and the fact of choice, by relating the satisfaction to personal ideals, enhances and may transform its quality. A prisoner may have all his basic needs met according even to some objectively determined optimum, and yet have little enjoyment from any of them, no one would claim that the satisfactions were on the same level for him in regard to any one of them as for a free man with full exercise of choice. So that if the set of circumstances of a physical order to which man is subject has general validity, it depends for its every application upon the particular channels of individual experience. Each needs food but the satisfaction he derives from a particular kind of food may well depend on his own particular ideas about it. Each fears ill-health or poverty or death but will suffer these fears in different quality and quantity according to his make-up and experience, and will seek to make his own pattern of adjustment to them.

The utilitarian method is here of special relevance for it brings out the importance of individual scales of preference approached by way of the pleasures and pains attached by each individual to particular satisfactions and dissatisfactions. And it is apparent that men do aim at maximizing the one and minimizing the other, that insofar as they are able to control these physical conditions, they seek happiness thus defined.

Discussion of these physical conditioning elements of the good life thus brings us on to a psychological plane where ideas and the interpretation of experience become a determining factor, and so constitute a second conditioning element. While to talk of the good life in the context of physical want or ill-health may seem to be divorced from reality, and there are basic needs which it is a necessary preliminary to satisfy, these themselves are seen to be not determinate objects of uniform shape. Rather does their particular manifestation vary with variations of constitution and experience in the subject. Ideas influence the form they take and the procedures through which they can be satisfied. These ideas may derive from the attitudes, customs, and traditions of the group, but they are modified by the constitution and experience of the individual. Thus the conditioning elements of a physical character do not govern in a direct and predetermined way the amount of happiness or self-fulfilment achieved. They have a bearing upon this but it is not one of simple cause and effect. Better health or more wealth does not necessarily mean more of happiness, fulfilment, or the good life. They only form part of the conditioning field, the other part depending on valuations—in short, on mental processes which attach meaning, make adaptations, determine uses. There is a point, that it so say, at which the conditioning elements are susceptible to direction and control. And it is only here that it begins to be possible to give substance to the concept of the good life. For this rests not only on an intelligent assessment of needs and satisfactions and of the whole 'situation' into which they fit, but on a directive activity which seeks to create a harmony between ideals co-ordinating desires and practice yielding fulfilment.

For while man is restricted by his own physical and environmental limitations, he is also a being of purpose seeking to bend them as far as is in his power to a pattern that commends itself to him. The good life is a concept involving compatibility between ideas, in the shape of that purposive pattern, and the conditions of behaviour. It occurs when aspirations fit opportunities, is absent when there is a misfit. If group life must be developed on the basis of action, behind action and necessarily harmonizing with it are beliefs and the standards by which they are judged. Delinquency, Sprott tells us, 'will be reduced only if society is so transformed that what is held up as worth living for can be achieved by the majority of the population.'[1]

The concept of self-realization, as we find it in political thinkers from Green to Hobhouse and Laski, expresses essentially this idea of adaptation. That is to say, it suggests a unity or harmony between two elements, the one belonging to the realm of mental, the other to that of physical, activity; the one to ideas, the other to behaviour. It does not imply, of course, of the former any relegation to an unreal world of mind dwelling apart in an ivory tower of idealistic super-reality, but on the contrary rests mental activity both on physical experience and in the processes of its actualization in language.[2] It properly places mental activity in the physical structure of the individual. Now it is perfectly true that many of those who have held to this concept of self-realization in one form or other have also sought to find a unity in minds that could explain away the fact of their evident differences in the conclusions or purposes that they reached. This, if it could be found, would resolve the difficulty of actually observed conflict which constitutes a central problem of politics. While they have clearly thought of this harmony between the two elements as the clue to the good life, they have claimed a unity of content for the mental element which they have derived from a metaphysical Idea activating it, whose existence cannot be empirically tested but rests upon an act of faith. Thus Thomas Aquinas said that 'the perfection of virtue results from the conformity of habit with reason', but this reason, though human and therefore variable in its manifesta-

[1] W. J. H. Sprott, *Science and Social Action* (1954).
[2] It is thus compatible with G. Ryle's account of this in his *The Concept of Mind* (1949).

tion, could only be used as a reliable measure inasmuch as it reflected divine reason.[1] Much the same is true of the 'idea' of which T. H. Green was thinking when he wrote that 'self-satisfaction is for ever sought and found in the realization of a completely articulated or thoroughly filled idea of the perfection of the human person'.[2] This applies too to Aristotle, and it is worth observing that we here find also an expression of a connection which continually recurs after him between the notion of self-realization or virtue and that of satisfaction or happiness. 'Let us acknowledge,' he wrote, 'that each one has just so much of happiness as he has of virtue and wisdom, and of virtuous and wise action. God is a witness to us of this truth; for he is happy and blessed, not by reason of any external good, but in himself and by reason of his own nature.'[3] When we speak here, however, of individual mental activity in which is generated purpose or an idea of good, with which conduct must be in harmony for the good life to be achieved, we are not assuming for the moment any necessary generality in its outcome or content. What is general lies instead in the structure or the process. It is an empirical and descriptive statement, that the good life is conceived as consisting in harmony between the two elements. Without claiming any necessary uniformity for the former, it suggests the need rather to examine the variations of content that are given by the expression of different thoughts or that can be gleaned from different courses of conduct. From agreement among those only can any generality be built, or incompatibilities be reconciled through institutions of co-operation. By reason both of their aspirations to rationality and of the community of experience from which such appraisals spring, it is to be expected that there will be considerable agreement, and even what may be called a developing moral purpose. Ginsberg produces cogent evidence for this; but in the last resort it remains true that 'only in terms of agreement and disagreement between persons is there any sense in the notion of "validity" ', and that if the holder of a belief 'can find no one to accept the particular standard he wishes to apply to a

---

[1] Jourdain, *Philosophie de Saint Thomas* (1858), Vol. I, p. 355.
[2] *Works*, Vol. II, p. 329.
[3] *Politics*, Vol. VII, pp. 1–10.

particular hypothesis, then it may remain valid for him, and for no one else'.[1]

Now, as has already been noted, there are signs of agreement, or at least of an association, between such concepts as those of the good life, self-realization, and of happiness. Certainly in the minds of philosophers we find that the ideas of goodness and happiness are closely linked; indeed that they are often all but co-terminous concepts. For the moment let us take only two examples from otherwise generally opposite schools of thought, although we shall refer to others later. Spinoza is one instance, with the argument that 'virtue is its own reward, in the strict sense that the best life is necessarily the happiest life'.[2] Or again, 'Particular pleasures in the narrow sense (*titillatio*) may be excessive, as upsetting the balance and well-being of the whole organism; but pleasure in the sense of conscious well-being and enjoyed activity is the characteristic of the free or intelligent man's life; to act well is fully to enjoy oneself and fully to enjoy oneself is to act well'.[3] And we can take as a second instance so different a philosopher as Bishop Butler. That strong advocate of the pre-eminence of conscience as the authoritative guide to conduct could constantly stress this same link between goodness and happiness. 'In the common course of life, there is seldom any inconsistency between our duty and what is called interest: it is much seldomer that there is any inconsistency between our duty and what is called interest; meaning by interest happiness and satisfaction. Self-love, then, . . . does in general perfectly coincide with virtue, and leads us to one and the same course of life.'[4] And he similarly finds in self-love and benevolence a common source both of goodness and of happiness.[5]

(b) *Happiness*

When we seek to discover, as a matter of observed fact, what are the ends that men set themselves to which the state is relevant, the state being intelligible only as an instrument for

[1] Sprott, *op. cit.*, p.
[2] Stuart Hampshire, *Spinoza* (1951), p. 164.
[3] *Ibid.*, p. 163.
[4] Austin Duncan-Jones, *Butler's Moral Philosophy* (1952), p. 47.
[5] *Ibid.*, p. 66.

fulfilling the purposes of its members, we seem invariably to be brought back to this linking of the ideas of good and happiness. This should dispose us to the belief that there is something in utilitarianism after all despite subsequent tendencies to dismiss it for its psychological crudities or its excessive claims. This may dispose us, too, to consider whether it can be restated in a way that avoids these while yet contributing something helpful to the understanding of what men seek. For it seems to be true that man regards as good what makes him happy and that he is happy only when doing what he regards as good.

The validity of this idea does not seem to have been impaired by subsequent criticism of utilitarianism, which has often been directed to confusions in its exposition or even to misinterpretations, springing from the ambiguous notion of pleasure. Thus we may say of one man that he was entirely given over to a life of pleasure and of another that his greatest pleasure was in denying himself for the benefit of others,[1] meaning quite different things by pleasure in the two cases, although there is also something common to both. The utilitarian principle when it equates the greatest amount of pleasure with the greatest happiness need refer no more to the former than to the latter use of this word, but rather to the common characteristic. Bentham himself certainly used it in this neutral sense. In effect, he said: you are to regard as pleasure whatever a man regards as a satisfaction or pleasure for him, and that is for him the good.

There are also, however, other assertions often alleged to invalidate this thesis which may reasonably be treated as no more than refinements of it. One, suggested by Hobhouse, is that man does not seek pleasure consciously but that he is moved by impulse with which no anticipation of an end is necessarily connected, although the impulse is modified by experience of the consequences in such a way as to encourage those which lead to pleasant ones, that is ones with which a pleasant tone of feeling is accompanied, this pleasure then consisting of a harmony between experience and feeling or object and means. Other criticisms are connected with the

[1] Or, as Burton, Bentham's editor, wrote, a man may be 'said to pursue pleasure to the destruction of his happiness'. Bentham, *Theory of Legislation* (ed. by Ogden), p. 501.

analysis of happiness, one being that happiness is not achieved by pursuing it directly, but that it is a by-product of the fulfilment of other purposes; another being that happiness is not a sum of pleasure as the utilitarians reckoned it, but rather a state of the whole nature and personality, a condition of mind, as Hobhouse has it, having the same feeling-tone as pleasure but not merely a series of pleasurable conditions. But none of these assertions really undermines the basic idea of linking good and happiness although they may make a valuable refinement of it. For the manner in which men seek or gain happiness does not matter in this connection provided happiness, regarded as enjoyed experience, is either the fundamental element in the end pursued or a necessary condition of the pursuit to make it worth while.

It is said for instance that we may pursue truth for its own sake, but it is obvious that we derive pleasure both from the acquisition of truth and from its pursuit. Conversely, we suffer discomfort from the thought that our understanding or information is false. And there can surely be no doubt that the underlying reason in both cases is that we need to be able to interpret the world about us in order the better to achieve our purposes in it, and that we recognize that a false interpretation hampers or precludes such achievement. Knowledge, as Bacon said, is power. Admitting that 'the love of truth may force us to change very comforting beliefs for very depressing ones',[1] we must reply that the former lose their power to comfort once their truth is doubted. Admitting again that we seek the development of ideals, that is the rational interpretation of experience in terms of purpose, and that the good can be defined as the application of these, it still seems to be the case that happiness lies in that application. So if we accept, as we seem therefore bound to do, that in seeking the good life man seeks happiness the method and condition of its achievement becomes the matter of most importance. And in analysing these we shall surely be doing something to elucidate our ideas about the basic elements of a political and social theory which falls into

[1] J. M. E. MacTaggart, *Studies in Hegelian Cosmology* (1918), p. 121, in his admirable discussion of the question whether the development of ideals is necessarily conducive to happiness. This argument also covers his view that wider sympathy may make us suffer more, if wider sympathy is part of the good from which happiness is derived.

its proper place as supplying a rational groundwork of political and social institutions. We need not claim that we are establishing a golden rule from which answers to political problems can be deduced, but only that this is in fact the sort of way in which the justification of functions performed by the state is usually made in current discussion.

This of course does not carry us far. The proposition that men seek happiness is too vague as it stands. Only when we bring it down to applications can we examine its significance. Such a process of application involves first the consideration of questions of how happiness is achieved or increased, of methods and conditions. And this is where doubts and difficulties arise. The primitive tribe imposes taboos directed by belief in the efficacy of magic, the advanced society develops a system of justice based on scientific principles; yet both may be seeking to increase happiness according to their lights. In what manner are we to suggest how and why one is likely to succeed more than the other?

The process of applying the proposition involves, secondly, questions of distribution. Happiness must be somebody's happiness, and we need to know whose. If my good is my own happiness, society's good may be that of a special group or of the greatest number, and this greatest number may be composed according to different principles of selection. A man may not be interested in the happiness of others but only in his own, or he may increase his own happiness through a willingness to make sacrifices for that of the greatest number. Such problems reveal the conflicts within social relationships, to which the proposition does not suggest that there is necessarily an answer, for it does not help us to choose between the happiness of one and of another, or even of several, on any final grounds. While the conflict remains as an actual or potential element in all systems of social co-operation, we are entitled, however, to draw some conclusions which may mitigate it. We can point to the fact that the social character of man exerts a constant pressure extending his idea of happiness in the direction of one of general happiness. And we can suggest that happiness is demonstrably greater the more it comprehends the good of others, the less it is narrowly selfish, and that more happiness attaches to 'a human being dissatisfied than a pig satisfied . . .

a Socrates dissatisfied than a fool satisfied'. Nor is there quite that unwillingness to admit differences in the qualities of pleasure frequently attributed to Benthamite utilitarianism. Did not Bentham himself emphasize such factors influencing 'the value of a pleasure' as, not only intensity and duration, but the extent to which it 'is likely to be followed by other pleasures', i.e. its 'productivity', and 'the number of persons who are likely to find themselves affected'?[1] There is also J. S. Mill's argument: 'To those who have neither public nor private affections, the excitements of life are much curtailed, and in any case dwindle in value as the time approaches when all selfish interests must be terminated by death: while those who leave after them objects of personal affection, and especially those who have also cultivated a fellow-feeling with the collective interests of mankind, retain as lively an interest in life on the eve of death as in the vigour of youth and health.'[2] If indeed we agree, on the whole, that altruism is preferable to selfishness, this idea seems to arise from the belief that it means more happiness in the long run.

We can now return to considering what we mean by the achievement of happiness, leaving aside at this point the second line of discussion which we have been following, that dealing with the distribution of happiness or the conflicting claims of the individual and of social groups. It has brought us to the conclusion that while in the last resort conflict remains, and so can only be resolved by some practical compromise, there are nevertheless strong forces in individual character as well as in social life making for agreement. We can accept that 'gregariousness and social adaptability are not the antithesis of self-interest but only the urge to self-preservation in its corporate aspect, and we can see no reason for according it any superior moral significance on that account'.[3] Thus the ways and conditions in which self-interest can be translated in terms of increasing happiness have a certain pre-eminence of claim to analysis.

It is true that there may often appear to be opposition between pursuit of men's declared objectives—such as truth,

---

[1] See, e.g. *Theory of Legislation* (Ogden edn.), p. 31.
[2] *Utilitarianism*, 1863, pp. 14, 20.
[3] K. Walter & P. Fletcher, *Sex and Society*, 1955, p. 62.

love, beauty, or conformity with some ideal system by surrender of their will to it—and their immediate happiness. It is true too that they may seem to be sacrificing happiness for something which they deem more fundamental. But that such opposition is superficial is suggested by their tendency to justify the sacrifice on the ground that they are replacing an immediate satisfaction by a greater or more enduring happiness. Thus Hurrell Froude, for example, after fasting and abstinences so bitter that they were affecting his health, could record in his Journal that he used such self-denial 'because I believe it the way to make the most out of our pleasures; and, besides, it has a tendency to give me what is essential to taking my place in society, self-command'.[1]

(c) *Utilitarianism*

This link between happiness and the good may be more Aristotelian than utilitarian but the association of it with satisfactions or pleasures is not—that is the idea of activity as directed to the maximizing of pleasure and the minimizing of pain and of the equivalence of happiness with the 'ultimate and permanent effects' of this.[2] Now it is this essential feature of utilitarianism which Sidgwick is sometimes said to have abandoned because he recognized the existence of disinterested or extra-regarding impulses to action. Of course, if we imagine the basis of utilitarianism to have been a hedonism which limits the motives of action to the agent's pleasure in the narrowest sense of direct satisfaction, sought regardless of others and of all other values, it is patently false. But Bentham's utilitarianism was never like that. He included 'the pleasures of the soul' in physical pleasures.[3] And he regarded the individual agent as an essentially social being. That being so, we are then bound to admit, what is surely obvious, and what was certainly admitted

---

[1] Geoffrey Faber, *Oxford Apostles* (1954), p. 209. Sir G. Faber continues: 'If this was not altogether true, it was certainly true that his motives were mixed. It pleased his vanity to be able to control his appetites. It was a time-honoured way of pleasing God, or at any rate by fitting the soul to please God better. It was also perhaps, a pleasure in itself. . . . The idea of fasting had a curious attraction, all its own.'

[2] Cf. J. Bentham, *Works*, Vol. I, p. 22.

[3] Cf. *Theory of Legislation* (Ed. Ogden), p. 502.

by Bentham, that he often derives pleasure from disinterested action, or what Bentham called benevolence.

When we go on to look more closely at the nature of this disinterested action we find it impossible to deny that it too is influenced by the desire to gain pleasure. The difference is that in this case the pleasure has two aspects; that enjoyed by another must be added to that which is enjoyed by the agent himself. As has been suggested already in discussing the neutral sense of pleasure—as meaning whatever gives satisfaction to the agent regardless of all other considerations—there does not appear to have been any logical necessity imposing the exclusion of those types of pleasure that are derived from disinterested motives or, at the other extreme, that are anti-social. On the contrary, we have the authority of Bentham himself who gave a high place on his list of pleasures to those of friendship and of the social affections, and who said of the pleasures of benevolence that 'they have the power of concentrating themselves into a narrow circle, or of spreading over entire humanity. Benevolence extends itself to animals of which we love the species or individuals; the signs of their happiness affect us agreeably.'[1] It is true, however, that this may not have been clearly enough stated or kept in view. Partly as a consequence of this the narrow conception of pleasure often became equated with the utilitarian view, which was thus accepted as being based upon this crude psychological hedonism. And so, as this could be shown to be an inadequate explanation of behaviour, utilitarianism itself could be discredited.

But partly the reason lay in quite a different field. This was the claim that the pleasure-pain or felicific calculus not only provided an explanation of what the individual judged desirable and pursued in his behaviour, and so also provided a reasonably satisfactory test of the objective of social morality, that is of what a group will judge desirable and how it will attempt to determine what he ought to do.[2] Not only was it true that he did pursue his own happiness, but it followed from this that, by some mysterious alchemy of a natural harmony of interests, if each obeyed this imperative, the greatest

[1] *Theory of Legislation* (Ed. Ogden), p. 22.
[2] For generally one of the best discussions of this see L. T. Hobhouse, *The Elements of Social Justice*, Ch. I.

happiness of the greatest number would result. By including this unproved metaphysical assumption the greatest happiness principle was elevated into an absolute, an objective criterion for testing morals and legislation and yielding certitudes.

Utilitarianism has indeed come to have so many different meanings that it may be as well to consider here what in it remains acceptable. First, we surely do in fact start both as children and as primitive men by equating good with our own pleasure. Some such initial equation takes place in all of us. But as has been said, it would be absurdly unrealistic to suppose that such pleasure was necessarily 'selfish'. On the contrary, owing to affection, sympathy, imagination, the feelings of other people are so immediately mixed up with our own that our own pleasure may often be better secured through serving theirs, and we begin very early in our experience to learn this fact. While it is true of course that in common language we habitually make the distinction between selfish and unselfish actions or people, we mean not that one is more concerned with pleasure than the other, but rather that the influence of affection, sympathy and imagination is less in one case than the other. No one thinks that the selfish person has more pleasure than the unselfish; rather is the contrary true; and to assume that the one pursues his own pleasure while the other does not leads only to confusion. Since to most, and probably to all, people there are many disinterested actions which produce more pleasure than a 'selfish' one, the recognition of disinterested impulses does nothing to deny the idea that we equate good with our own pleasure.

So we may continue by saying that this simple equation will very soon need modifying by the recognition that 'our own pleasure' is a much more complex thing than may at first sight appear. We rapidly learn lessons in connection with it as our experience of living with others expands. The first is its disinterested content, the pleasures of altruism, of service, of enjoying the happiness of another; or conversely we discover the discomfort that we can suffer through the pain or unhappiness of another. This might be called the passive aspect of the reaction upon ourselves because it is not due to any action of that other directed upon us. The child, for instance, may enjoy the happiness or suffer the sadness which it has caused its parent, regardless of any question of reward or punishment. But the second lesson is no less important. We also learn about rewards and punishments, that the effect of doing something which gives us pleasure may be to annoy and so to induce actions from which we suffer. This, the active aspect of the reaction, will also modify the simplicity of our equation. We seek not only our own happiness but a way of living with others that will make our happiness continuously possible. Which introduces the third lesson—that of dimension in time. We demand of pleasure more than momentary satisfaction, being always in some measure conscious of the future in the present, and aware of the alloy constituted by the mutability of things. We seek enduring pleasure and are comforted in pain by the thought that it will pass. This is the case whether the remoter consequences spring directly from our enjoyment or result from the intervention of others induced thereby. The former consideration led the stoic to advocate the limitation of pleasures as a means of avoiding the pains of privation on denial of them. The latter is exemplified by any course of action which is likely to cause retaliation by others. In short, we progress from the short-sighted demand for immediate gratifications to the more far-sighted search for a pattern of living that will secure the possibility of continuing happiness.

Thus our analysis does not move from the idea of a simple and momentary pleasure equation to a greatest happiness of the greatest number principle but from a complex pleasure or happiness idea, which takes full account of its disinterested or altruistic or social content, to the recognition of the necessity for its accommodating itself to the needs and desires of others as they also seek their happiness. We seek, that is to say, that way of living with others or that kind of society which we prefer, and we prefer it because it gives us most chance of happiness, regarded as a way of living that maximizes pleasure over a continuous process of time.

So we learn that our pleasure and, still more, our happiness is not only involved in that of others, but must to some extent comprehend it, and is in large measure dependent upon it. Thus the pursuit of our own happiness requires some pursuit of that of some others. With the growth of sympathy, imagination, and social consciousness, there is a widening circle of those in whose happiness we recognize our own as being involved. That is not to say that we arrive directly at the principle of pursuing the greatest happiness of all. For we certainly do not regard the happiness of an unknown person as an equally compelling objective with the happiness of someone we love. We are also influenced by the practical question how much we ourselves can do to promote the happiness of another. But we do in fact extend the objective from the self through an inner circle of those for whom we have special affection into a much wider comprehensiveness. The process, however, is one of such extension. No more is necessary to explain it, though it is aided and supported by the awareness that others also desire and need their own happiness, are pursuing it similarly, and that there is thus an interlocking of individual objectives. The need for them to be brought into the greatest possible harmony clearly becomes, therefore, the guide to the institutions of social or political co-operation. We may assert too that this process of extension is aided and supported by the 'principle' of reciprocity which we get from the experience of living with others, an idea of fair exchange and of 'do as you would be done by'. It is assuredly in this manner that the purpose of general happiness is built up as an acknowledged chief objective of social co-operation, and there is no need to bring in, as Sidgwick did, an intuition that it is right according to some prior and pre-established order of morality. It may be that we simply mistake for an 'intuition' what is really a telescoping of the longer rational process of appraisal which we have been here outlining.

That is to say that we do not accord approval for the greatest happiness principle on the basis of an intuition that it is an absolute and objective moral imperative, but rather to suggest that our own experience leads us, by way of the extension just described, to regard it as the most valid guide to a programme of social co-operation because it establishes the foundations of a society in which we may expect, or most reasonably hope, that others will do as we want. This is a society which we prefer inasmuch as it gives us most chance of living according to our own ideas and purposes, or our *weltanschauung*. But there is no endorsement in this of the definition of what we want as momentary pleasure narrowly and shortsightedly conceived at the expense of our sympathies, our need of others, and our own future happiness.

Thus joined to the view, fundamentally utilitarian, that the explanation of purpose in behaviour is the search for happiness, are two others which have been wrongly considered inconsistent with it, but which may be regarded as necessary elaborations of it. The first is that the principle, pursue your own pleasure as the greatest good, is perfectly compatible with what Archbishop Temple called 'the higher selfishness'. Indeed it is obvious that much sound guidance on how most successfully to apply this principle is to be found in the teaching of religions, not least the Sermon on the Mount. It may well be that to love your neighbour as yourself is the surest way to happiness or that the service of others affords the greatest pleasure. The important point, however, is that if such is the fact it requires no further validation. Out of the experience of what gives us satisfaction we create our philosophy of life; it is built, that is to say, on the idea of happiness. But secondly we find that, man being a creature of ideas and purpose, he acts on the belief that his behaviour ought to reflect them. Indeed we may say that men normally make the assumption that their actions ought to be in harmony with their idea of good. With experience they are found to be continually modifying either the one or the other in order to bring them into harmony. For it is clear that they also derive a certain kind of satisfaction from such harmony: more, that they require it as a condition of their peace of mind. Which is another way of saying that for happiness there must be a conformity of act and idea, behaviour and philosophy, or conduct and experience. Thus does the consideration of happiness enter into not only the content of the idea of good as its explanation but also into the application of the *weltanschauung* or practical philosophy as its result. So we can say that happiness requires both the creation of a personal *weltanschauung* built on all experience, including that of social life, and the harmonizing of behaviour or the way of life with it. And we may go on from this to claim that the more it comprehends of experience within it, the more rational or intelligent it is, the more will it be capable of yielding satisfaction.

If, then, it would seem that at least one of man's normal criteria of good is conduciveness to his own happiness, this criterion does not imply the unconsidered pursuit of every fleeting fancy, but rather the intelligent assessment of his whole situation, which comprises his own mental and physical nature and needs, his beliefs, and his relations with others.

IV

OBLIGATION AND COMMAND

BUT as we have said, such a utilitarianism as this does not imply the wholly different proposition that the general happiness principle can be established as an absolute moral imperative, the truth of which we perceive by intuition. Many today, it is true, would agree that the kind of society they prefer is one which acts on some such principle, or even that, if such a simple general guide is sought, they do not see a better one. But that is by no means to say that it will furnish us with a clear solution, and only one possible solution, to every practical problem, or tell us exactly what should be done in all circumstances. Indeed, the idea that such a single universal answer to all questions is necessary and possible may be regarded as a vestigial transcendentalism. It is a hangover from an attitude to morals and politics which sought to base authority on a supernatural absolute, and which is replaced by a view of the state as a co-operative association for the pursuit of the varying and sometimes conflicting purposes of its members.

This means that the source of moral directive or obligation must be within those purposes and not outside and above them. Now what is to be inferred from this is that if their own happiness is the guide to these 'purposes of its members', as being the good they aim at, such an idea of purpose necessarily contains the idea of obligation inasmuch as it indicates the criterion of judgment they accept. When they will the end they will the means, and in willing the end they accept the means as an imperative. When they express a preference they imply an obligation. In agreed preferences and the beliefs they rest on lies the sole basis of authority: in them is the source of obligation and command. Common acceptance alone can create a community.

The fact that we are thus making a transfer from indicative to imperative calls for some further remark. For at first sight it may appear to conflict with the principle accepted since Hume that it is logically impossible to infer 'ought' from 'is'. But it is only if, when we say that someone ought to do so and so, we are seeking to establish demonstrable rules, that this is the case. Here it is not, for we are not applying such rules. Rather are we appraising a situation and inferring consequences from preferences. If we say that our purpose is our happiness then we infer that our acts ought to be directed to our happiness. When we speak of purpose we are certainly not thinking of Plato's 'factual, existing good, knowable by a kind of supra-sensible observation'. Rather is it as 'Aristotle puts a "good to be achieved by action", or, as he usually calls it, an "end".' It is to claim with him that 'to say something is good is to guide action'.[1] If this is not to state a measurable fact about the world, it is to treat a preference or purpose as a fact and to infer other appraisals from it. Thus we are using the imperative in a way with which Weldon agrees when he writes: 'For in ordinary speech "You ought to do that", "That ought to be the case" refer to consequences and mean simply "It would be better if . . ." They concern appraisals which may or may not involve the keeping of rules. . . . Thus while it is correct to say that if we knew all the probable consequences of our acts, we should very seldom be in any doubt as to what we ought to do, this is not the same as to say that if we knew all the political and other rules, we should always know what we ought to do. . . . It is perfectly correct to say that only by intensive study of the facts can we reach sound appraisals and advise other people as to their best course of action';[2] and, indeed, it is in just the same way that we decide what we ourselves ought to do.

For, again, we are taking the making of a command as containing, as a necessary element in it, the expression of a wish, though necessarily also containing something more, namely that something be done. In issuing the command I do in fact want to affect causally the behaviour of the hearer—or of myself if I

[1] R. M. Hare, *The Language of Morals* (1952), p. 29.
[2] T. D. Weldon, *The Vocabulary of Politics* (1953), p. 191.

am also the hearer—in accordance with the wish behind it, and that wish alone makes sense of it. I cannot issue the command without having the wish. This is one of those theories which R. M. Hare says, in his *The Language of Morals*, he is 'not seeking to refute. They have all of them the characteristic that, if put in everyday terms, they say nothing exceptionable so far as their main contentions go'; but they are not, he says, helpful for resolving philosophical perplexities. So we are taking the matters with which we are here concerned as capable of being satisfactorily dealt with in 'everyday terms' rather than 'philosophical' ones. His contention is that when I say 'Shut the door' I am doing something quite different from what I am doing when I say 'I wish you to shut the door', and 'it would be perverse to explain the meaning of the imperative mood in terms of wishing . . . for we learn how to respond to and use commands long before we learn the comparatively complex notions of "wish", "desire", "aversion", etc.' Some might think, however, that whether or not we learn the notion of 'wish' or 'desire' before or after we learn to respond to commands, we certainly are conscious of the thing itself at the very earliest stage before even we have learnt to express it in language. But what is of practical interest and importance is the relation between the wish behind the command and the effecting of it in action. It may also involve, especially for politics, questions at the middle stage of how a wish becomes a command, of the authority belonging to the issuer of the command or of the prospects of its being obeyed; all of which would seem to be rendered more difficult to ask or solve if the necessity of the connection is denied. For they may belong to the field of social relationships where the expectation of the wish having an effect on action will depend upon that relationship. It is one of the assumptions of a democratic representative system of government that the command of the government reflects the wishes of the majority. They wish for a public health service; the government issues the commands which will effect their purpose. Both are prescriptions; though they differ in the process and certainly of their implementation. For Henry II to wish to be rid of Becket may cause the latter to be murdered. The command 'shut the door' may be less effective in getting the door shut if the grounds for authority are absent or not accepted by the hearer than would be the wish statement, and for political purposes that may be the important point.

But what matters here is that this brings out the connection between appraisals producing preferences and wishes producing commands. Hare classifies both commands and moral judgments as prescriptions. Here we treat both as expressing a wish or preference for bringing something about—a wish or preference, that is, which has the character of prescribing it or saying that it ought to be brought about. It is in this sense that we are moving from the indicative to the imperative.

How can we describe the process of approval or condemnation which lies behind the idea of obligation and command, and also plays an important part in the formation of purpose? Partly it is conative, partly cognitive. It represents both an emotional reaction of liking or disliking and a judgment in which reasoning has its place. Each is conditioned by personal experience and influenced by attitudes current in the society to which we belong. If a twentieth century Englishman is told that 'Smith beats his wife', his immediate inclination will be to condemn Smith. He will feel an emotional reaction of intense dislike. Were he then told that had he lived in the time of Pepys he would not have suffered such sensations, and were he then asked therefore to explain the grounds for his condemnation he could not be content with a mere statement that it is 'not done', or that there has been a change in attitude to the position of married women, of which alterations in the divorce and property laws are symptomatic. He would want to show why such a change in attitude was an improvement, claiming, for instance, that, while it deprived the husband of something, what he gained more than compensated, and that in the long run it was likely to be more conducive to his happiness because it made possible a more satisfying companionship; that the wife has just as good a claim to personal security and happiness as the husband; that on the assumption that she does not want to suffer, or to go about in fear of suffering, violence, the change was conducive to her happiness also, though if the assumption were wrong the conclusion would be wrong too. Or he might generalize more widely and argue that all violence is bad, that appeal to the arbitrament of force militates against rational decision; that the use of force is as contrary to the interests in the long run of the person who uses it as in the short run to those of its victim; or even, more broadly still, that there is a *prima facie* case for regarding cruelty of any kind and at all times as bad, in the belief that it can never be conducive to happiness.

Now from such an account of the process of approval or condemnation—or moral appraisal—two points of some significance emerge. The first is that it deals with anticipated consequences and expresses a judgment, which may be correct or incorrect, in terms of these. It is not the enunciation of an absolute principle which is accepted *a priori* and then applied to all situations. The second is that, while it takes the form of generalizing, and indeed men must generalize their ideas of good in their search for an orderly interpretation of experience upon which they can communicate with one another, it is a generalizing which each makes from his own experience, direct or inter-learned. And when he approves or condemns in the case of the actions of another he does so in terms of the effects primarily on that other, and then of those most immediately affected. Such is the manner of the proceeding whereby he arrives at an assertion which is at once generalized and an imperative, having the form 'it is desirable that' or 'it ought to be'. Thus such an analysis as this means that when a man judges good the action—or the total of actions which is the character—of another, he means that it is marked by what, generalizing from his own experience, he would judge to be conducive to a satisfactory way of living for that other. It is only to the extent that his own experience or 'situation' is similar to that of another that he will claim it issues in a similar assessment. And this is surely what men in fact do when they make such judgments. They relate them to consequences and to differences in 'situation'. They put themselves imaginatively into the situation, which includes the capacities and beliefs, of another. They do not say, for instance, that the non-swimmer should dive to the assistance of a drowning man, or that the Mahommedan should eat pork. The statesman may have these problems in a peculiarly dramatic form owing to their scale. When President Truman had to decide whether to use the atomic bomb, an act of cruelty on a colossal and unprecedented scale, he had to set the effects on the people of Hiroshima and Nagasaki against the desire of even larger numbers in armies, prospective invasion areas, prisoner of war camps, and indeed of immense civilian populations to live out their lives in security. As its use led in fact to a speedy end of the war and can be claimed with some degree of certainty to have reduced the total of suffering in succeeding months and years, there has probably been much more approval than condemnation of it in the world at large, not excluding Japan. But had the effects been different, so might the judgment have been, although the motives would have been the same. There can be no certitude in such matters of a kind which would spring from the existence of absolute principles, clear and unchanging and only awaiting application.

In arguing in this way that principles or 'objective standards' depend upon acceptance by individual judgment applying empirical tests, we may be accused of subjectivism. There is no need to quarrel with that. For we do indeed say that the most important element in the judgment that something is good, or in the act of approving it, is that we like it, taking account of all it involves. But that is by no means to say that we cannot give reasons for doing so nor that these are not a necessary part of the judgment. A moral principle is not merely a matter of personal taste, although this is a much greater part of it than is admitted by most authorities. Once again, as with the distinction between a command and a wish, our criticism of these authorities is that the logical contrast they attempt to draw is too complete. When they contrast matters of taste, about which there can be no argument, with matters of principle, which are based on reason, they seem to be exaggerating in both instances.

To use an example of Bertrand Russell's, I may like oysters and you may not, but this does not mean that I cannot give reasons for doing so, nor that you may not persuade me to dislike them by telling me something about their habits or the effects of eating them. For taste is affected by experience. We can change our tastes, we may 'acquire' a taste, through a new experience. This process of acquiring is often influenced by the report given to us by others of their experience. Our tastes are influenced by our knowledge and thought; so new information or arguments may alter them. But in the final outcome it is true that taste is a matter of personal decision although it generally makes sense to ask for reasons for it.

Much the same, however, may be said of a matter of moral principle. If I judge it right to relieve Smith's poverty I am not applying an absolute principle of charity whose authority is objective in the sense that it exists within itself without argument and is of universal validity. I am making a concrete decision for which, again, it makes sense to demand reasons. But when these reasons are analysed it will always be found that they contain an element of personal preference. They will reduce to such statements as that I do not like the idea of his starving, or that I prefer a society in which men such as Smith are not left to starve, or in which no one starves, and I can go on giving reasons.

Now these preferences are facts and there is agreement in holding many of them. This agreement gives them the authority of numbers or even of the generality of their acceptance. From such facts of preference and of agreement thereon we can claim that the principles in which they emerge contain a certain stability, and it is this stability which it is perfectly admissible to characterize as giving them objectivity, provided we admit its dependence upon the processes of individual judgment which give it its basis in fact. They are based on an appeal to the processes of reasoning from our preferences to the conditions upon which these can be made effective, and not to an abstract and super-sensible Reason. But such preferences do not, it is true, belong to the world of metrically measurable fact, or to which 'either . . . or' statements are generally relevant. 'This sort of statement,' as Weldon says of appraisals, 'is just as checkable by reference to observed facts as "He is red-headed", but it does not give the same kind of information; it is not checkable by the same simple technique, and it is on the whole more subject to error and therefore more a matter on which there may be differences of opinion between different observers.'[1] We do not need to be afraid of what he calls the subjective bogey.

But there is no need, either, to go to the other extreme of saying that because there is no proof for the metaphysical foundations of democracy in which many political thinkers have believed, or because such founding principles are so vague that they may mean anything or nothing, that therefore it is impossible to talk significantly about foundations at all.

[1] T. D. Weldon, *The Vocabulary of Politics* (1953), p. 153.

On the contrary, we can claim of, for instance, the proposition that 'Men are always to be treated as ends and never as means' that it has no need of metaphysical justification. The notion that it does springs, as we have already argued, from wrong definitions of the state. For if they are to be treated as means then it must be to some end which has some metaphysical explanation. And it is a matter of observable fact that they do regard themselves as ends. Nor is such a proposition as useless in its practical implications as Weldon suggests when he asserts that it tells us 'nothing whatever about how to deal with prisoners of war, criminals, or taxi-drivers'.[1] Certainly if we are to treat them as means to, say, the power of the state we may well deal with them quite differently, and without involving ourselves in any of the considerations of purpose, happiness, conditions of co-operation put forward here.

In fact, however, we regard neither the objectivist nor the subjectivist definition as adequate but both as containing an element of truth, for both indicate the way in which we seek to reach moral conclusions, though neither guarantees finality or produces 'proof'.

Man is not naturally good or naturally evil, even though it be true to say that he naturally seeks his own happiness. If we define good as that which is generally approved it is misleading to say that there is some force impelling all men to seek it, for there are many who patently do not. The belief in the doctrine of original sin is equally misleading: men are not bound by an unregenerate past to do that which they generally condemn, although they may often fall short of their ideals. If, on the other hand, we were to define good subjectively as for anyone that which he approves, then perhaps the former, or humanist, view of 'natural goodness' would be truer to the facts.

The psychoanalyst tells us that the unconscious mind is the seat both of impulses and desires without moral direction and of a repressive force or censor which may not be rational at all. It is only at the conscious level that there enters the rational process of moral approval. It is here that, as Dewey says,[2] 'intelligence converts desire into plans', and at this stage some element of approval must enter. For 'what intelligence has to do

[1] *The Vocabulary of Politics*, p. 97.
[2] *Human Nature and Conduct*, p. 255.

in the service of impulse is to act not as its obedient servant but as its clarifier and liberator. And this can be accomplished only by a study of the conditions and causes, the workings and consequences of the greatest possible variety of desires and combinations of desire.' The 'plans' which are the result of adopting 'the psychoanalytic method with its attempt to face and express (at least in words) all aspects of our nature'[1] are thus an intelligent appraisal of what is worth seeking, and entail approval. Ambiguity arises, however, owing to defects in this process of intelligent appraisal. For often such a simple conscious act of rational judgment is not fully made, and in that case a man may not know what he approves at least in any articulate form. Or he may not be willing to admit to approving the 'plans', which he nevertheless pursues, being prevented by some emotion or inhibition, convention, or social taboo. We may say that we approve of one thing and yet make a habit of doing the contrary, but surely in such a case what we say can hardly be accepted as expressing our fully considered judgment. It is much more like the irrational censor perhaps expressing a subconscious fear than an act of intelligence producing 'plans'. However, when these obscurities are removed from the process of intelligent appraisal and they are seen as an attempt to do what Dewey and the psychoanalyst describe, then it must be admitted that there is clearly the tendency at least for actions to be brought into harmony with 'plans', or for men to do what they regard as good.

It may be objected that this is to say that what men do must, because they do it, be what they regard as good. In that case why bother to call it good? But this is grossly to oversimplify. For 'plans' are built out of experience by a process of trial and error. They do not spring fully formed from a single act of reasoning, but grow being modified by lessons learnt in the very performance of them. They are never perfect and never succeed in meeting all requirements. Their resemblance is not to an engineer's blueprint, but rather to the design for a garden, which discoveries made in the operation of it about the characteristics of the soil, about the impracticability of combining different plants, or about better arrangements of them will be continually changing. Though the plan is never finally

[1] Flugel, *Man, Morals and Society*, p. 29.

good in itself and is constantly being adapted or improved, it does represent a process of aiming at a harmony which is approved and which will satisfy. Despite its never being finally good yet it is always relatively so as long as the aim at harmony and the tendency to express it are present.

And we can then perhaps also redefine the doctrine of original sin by equating sin with man's failure to conform to his 'plans', or failure to do what he approves, that is as 'missing his aim'. With that definition we must also admit all the weakness and stupidity through which he will fail to live in accordance with that he approves. If that is true individually it is of course also true collectively. But this is to assert not that such failure is due to the mystic force of evil working upon men, but rather to their inexperience, confusion or miscalculation, or to conflicting pulls in their nature, to the fact that they feel different needs all of which it is impossible to satisfy.

All the same men do in fact, of course, do evil things, evil in the sense of what is generally condemned. We have to take measures of self protection against the criminal. It is even the case that a whole society may commit collective atrocities or at least their rulers may commit them and society apparently acquiesce. When this occurs and we have a recalcitrant group or even nation thus throwing over 'the moral laws' have we no answer, no ethical principle of right, no ultimate verity or authority to which we can appeal? Though experts in ethics or philosophy may disagree as to why they think a thing good they nevertheless have little difficulty in arriving at a common identification of good in many, or even most, cases. Undoubtedly there is this body of widespread agreement, which may even reach to universal acceptance at a given time and place, but we should beware of ascribing to it therefore the quality of ultimate authority, or of claiming the right to enforce it on that ground, for we must never forget the subjective basis of moral judgment. On the other hand we are perfectly entitled to condemn and to take the measures necessary to prevent actions, whether by individuals, groups, or nations, which will make difficult or still more render impossible to other individuals, groups, or nations the living of the good life as they wish to define it for themselves. And this surely supplies all that is required in practice to justify our defence against 'evil'.

Nor is such an argument a hair-splitting, or a distinction without a difference for practical purposes. On the contrary, it is important for at least two reasons. In the systems of philosophy with which it contrasts, where the appeal is to external authority, men are exhorted to do what may often be the right things for the wrong reasons. And when this is the case, although it may be temporarily convenient to society because inducing conformity, it can never be satisfactory to themselves because it causes internal conflict between what is accepted and what is acted upon. For however widespread the agreement behind authority may be, what gives it its claim to obedience lies not in its objective essence, however widely supported, but in its acceptance by the subject. To demand conformity on the ground of authority rather than of reason is to set up a double source of command, to establish a potential conflict of purpose and so a split personality. This making of discipline into the end instead of the means has the effect of discouraging the integration of self-development. Nor can it be satisfactory to society in the long run. Indeed it is liable to defeat itself. For the more men are governed by intelligence the less will they be willing to conform to authority unsubmitted to intelligence. This will create or strengthen disunity in society. And so to escape the dilemma authority will be driven to discourage intelligence and thus to seek the basis for obedience in the quicksands of emotion, an invitation to decay or self-destruction.

Another reason for the practical importance of this distinction lies in the intimate connection, for which psychologists appear to be discovering increasing evidence, between this attitude of submission to intelligence rather than authority and the development of tolerance. Freedom and openness of mind engender both an internal security, which makes it natural to tolerate difference because there is no cause to fear it, and a willingness to criticize without hostility which provides a safe escape for instincts of aggression. Conversely their investigations suggest that the characteristics of prejudice and intolerance are associated with an authoritarian mental background. Here discipline and authority encourage fear and insecurity. Repressed beneath an outward conformity, which has never become a voluntary act, are hostility and aggression seeking satisfaction in prejudice and active intolerance, looking for scapegoats to blame rather than causes to rectify when anything goes wrong. In short it is inimical to the conditions of a successful system of social co-operation.

Besides, there is always the danger that we shall overestimate the certitude or the generality of acceptance attaching to the ultimate verity or authority to which we appeal. And this is especially so in a society of strong common beliefs. We are much more ready to take it upon ourselves to affirm moral judgments for others the nearer they are, or the more like we conceive them to be, to ourselves. 'Is it not strange,' wrote Lord Esher in 1880, 'that the English, who flatter themselves they can govern alien races better than any other nation on the earth's surface, should fail when they come to deal with Catholic Celts? If the Irish were Mahommedans or Hindus we should have no difficulty with them. Every consideration would be then shown to their religious prejudices. Because they are Catholics they have been treated like dogs and are borne down by the vulgar bigotry of English evangelicalism. Here in England, we insist, and we are entitled to do so, upon Protestant supremacy. We shall do no good in Ireland until we admit there the supremacy of the Catholics.'[1]

For the basis of authority lies in a common way of life and the common beliefs, attitudes, and ideas of purpose which go with it. These alone create a sense of community. The whole concept of authority relies on agreement as to ends. Concordant wishes or preferences issue in generally accepted laws, institutions, and policies: these are the social expression of 'plans'. The recognition of obligation, of the duty to obey and the right to command, springs from a unity of purpose or a sharing of ideals overriding lesser dissidences. Where such agreement vanishes and groups, or individuals, become more conscious of differences of purpose than of similarity, and are therefore no longer willing to co-operate in the state as an agreed way of settling them, the grounds for recognizing obligation are removed, and the disintegration of authority is on its way. Thus the source of obligation is once more seen to lie in the processes by which preferences take the form of moral judgments, and 'intelligence converts desire into plans'. The theme of such processes can be called reason and political purpose. Examining

[1] *Journals and Letters of Reginald, Viscount Esher* (1934), Vol. I, p. 76.

this will lead us to see the basis of morality, and so of authority or the admission of obligation, first in the individual, and then the social, formulation of purposes.

V

REASON
AND POLITICAL PURPOSE

WE have said that defining the state as a co-operative association means that questions about its purpose become questions about the purposes of its members. When we consider what can usefully be said about these we are confronted by the fact that they reflect needs and express desires. It is these, we saw, which intelligence converts into plans. To some extent, however, desires and needs can be met at the level of reflex action and direct emotional response, with scarcely the use of intelligence at all. This is true of the earliest satisfactions of the infant, and it applies to some adult satisfactions also. Similarly primitive man's life operates more on this plane of experience than does that of men living in civilized societies. But it is only when reflection is brought to bear on the facts of need and desire that we can properly speak of purpose. For purpose implies mental activity which, though it may have elements linking it with physical response, is readily distinguished from this. It exists only at the level where intelligence, using processes of reason and imagination, issues in directives for action to follow.

Thus we are not thinking of purpose simply as an end but as an end to be achieved in action, not merely as an objective but also as a way of reaching it, not only as a desire but as a plan, as a pattern of behaviour, or a way of life, for satisfying a combination of desires. Implicit in such an approach is the idea that activity should accord with plans for fulfilment to be achieved. Now, it is this idea which many have sought to make a foundation of political theory, and either a guiding principle, or a justifying one, for the democratic state. Some have called it self-realization, others fulfilment of personality, and there are further variants. Common to them all, as has been pointed out, is the idea of a harmony between ideal and application, between a mental process and a behavioural one; and the identification with virtue as well as happiness. The concept, however, is rightly said to lack precision. It is certainly one of those ideas which the recent critics of the seekers after foundations of political theory rightly allege to be incapable, as it stands, of providing clear deductions in the form of one, and one only, institutional expression of it. As J. C. Rees writes, 'Two persons who proclaimed their common allegiance to "fulfilment of personality" as the basic norm in moral valuation could not accuse each other of logical inconsistency if they held different conceptions of social justice. If they did they would be confusing a method of justification with a moral judgment and those who would defend the theory of human fulfilment against its modern critics in this manner are failing to make the same distinction.'[1] Nevertheless analysis of the concept which Rees criticizes can both give it greater precision and, while not attempting to establish it as a basic norm, can yet show it to have usefulness in clarifying ideas of political purpose and even in giving them a certain conceptual unity.

For there are two important points which this idea of self-realization serves to emphasize. The first is its basis in individual separateness. Each self, it argues, has its own peculiar system of mental activity, resembling, but never identical with, others, and operating on an accumulation, which is unique, of experiences whose sources are common, but whose character it is impossible ever to say is precisely the same. The second point lies in the use that each can make of his system of mental activity. For in the application of intelligence to environment he becomes the conscious moulder of his behaviour. This idea of conscious control is central to the concept of self-realization, which indeed takes man's potentiality for this to be his most distinctive characteristic. This is the free will assertion that inasmuch as man is not determined by external causes but controls his reactions to his environment and masters his environment itself is he rational or intelligent, and capable of virtue and happiness.

[1] *Loc. cit.*

This is in fact to start from Spinoza's statement that 'Each particular thing possesses a determinate nature of its own only insofar as it is active and not passive in relation to things other than itself, that is, only insofar as its status can be explained otherwise than as the effects of external causes.... Its character and individuality depends on its necessarily limited power, of self-maintenance; it can be distinguished as a unitary thing with a recognizable constancy of character insofar as, although a system of parts, it succeeds in maintaining its own characteristic coherence and balance of parts.'[1] J. S. Mill characterized individuality in much the same way. 'A person whose impulses are his own—are the expression of his own nature, as it has been developed and modified by his own culture—is said to have a character. One whose desires and impulses are not his own, has no character, no more than a steam-engine has a character.'[2] Indeed we can apply the extent of conscious control as a test of development: 'It becomes possible,' says Ginsberg, 'to use as a criterion of advance the degree to which control of the conditions of life is consciously guided or directed.'[3] This is to recognize in the mental process of reflection a guiding element in morality, and to see that the more there is conscious control of activity in harmony with ideals resulting from such reflection, the greater is the moral significance of activity. It is to assert that activity can only be given meaning through a mental process which interprets experience, brings order into it, and develops purpose from it. This, again, is what we mean by saying that it is rational. The more this process is consistent with itself and comprehensive, the greater is its potentiality for happiness. For happiness like morality cannot be imposed from outside. It is the result of internally developed harmony. We can agree with Dewey: 'To say that the welfare of others, like our own, consists in a widening and deepening of the perceptions that give activity its meaning, in an educative growth, is to set forth a proposition of political import. To "make others happy" except through liberating their powers and engaging them in activities that enlarge the meaning of life is to harm

---

[1] Stuart Hampshire, *Spinoza* (1951), p. 77.
[2] *Essay on Liberty* (World's Classics, 1924), p. 74.
[3] *Reason and Unreason in Society* (1947), p. 29.

them and to indulge ourselves under cover of exercising a special virtue.'[1]

Now the prime factor in this conscious control belongs to the mind, or the reason or whatever we may prefer to call that part or aspect of man which is capable of mental activity. Modern science denies the existence of mind as an entity separate from the body and has established the close interaction of mental and physical activity. It thus supports Hobhouse when he writes: 'The view here taken is that harmony is not a subjection of any part to any other, but a process of mutual development, and that reason does not govern this process *ab extra* but is the principle of mutuality within it',[2] although even here, since there must be, according to Hobhouse, a conformity with reason for harmony to exist, there is no real difference between his view and Plato's. There is no need to establish as separate and independent entities Plato's distinctive elements—reason, appetite, passion or the spirited element—in order to validate Plato's conception. The point of importance is the place of reason or the rational principle, however it may be derived, in relation to the other parts or elements: it is to decide whether it is in a governing position as determining the nature of the harmony which is a concept common to Plato and to Hobhouse, or whether it is merely as it were a co-equal element in that harmony. We do not need to follow Plato's poetic imagery by asserting that reason governs *ab extra* in order to establish the truth that reason, just because it is the principle of mutuality, is also the yardstick or principle of ultimate reference and therefore in very real sense is the governing principle as in Plato's argument. Hobhouse himself, when examining elsewhere the course by which reason comes to establish itself, implicitly admits its position as guiding principle, and a guiding principle is not very different from a governing principle. 'There are filaments of reason—,' he writes, 'but filaments are not the matured structure. They grow because they do, in fact, correspond to fundamental conditions of life, not because the life which they create is clearly conceived. Reason comes by her own, not because men willingly and consciously accept her, but because unreason carried far enough produces miseries and

[1] J. Dewey, *Human Nature and Conduct*, p. 293.
[2] *The Rational Good* (1921), p. 104.

disaster.'[1] Among more recent writers Gilbert Ryle also admits 'primacy of a certain sort' for 'intellectual powers, propensities, and performance.'[2]

This is not far removed from Plato and certainly is not incompatible with his rhetorical question: 'Is it not then essentially the province of the rational principle to command, inasmuch as it is wise, and has to exercise forethought on behalf of the entire soul, and the province of the spirited principle to be its subject and ally?'[3]

We find this line of thought applied both in ethics and in politics, to the government by man of his own conduct and to government within the state. Graham Wallas, for instance, points with approval to 'Plato's conception of the harmony of the soul—the intensification both of passion and of thought by their conscious co-ordination'.[4] We have here again the idea of conscious control or a submission to mental activity, or the reason. And he points out also, with similar approval, that 'Plato teaches that the supreme purpose of the state realizes itself in men's hearts by a "harmony" which strengthens the motive force of passion, because the separate passions no longer war among themselves, but are concentrated on an end discovered by the intellect'.[5]

Is it not clear that in any conception of the good life the reason must enter, man being a creature of purpose, and not an automaton moved by blind desires and impulses within himself or blindly reflecting forces external to him, and that if reason enters at all it can enter only as the element which gives meaning to experience, that is to internal desire and external force? To give meaning is to value and so to build purpose. It is therefore to give direction to activity. To co-ordinate into a harmony is in fact to govern. Hobhouse writes: 'The analysis of thought points to the conception of the reason as an impulse to secure harmony of conceptions, an impulse which can only be finally validated by development.'[6]

Nor is there any need to think of reason as existing in a

---

[1] *The Rational Good* (1921), p. 121.
[2] *The Concept of Mind* (1949), p. 280.
[3] *Republic*, IV, 441.
[4] *Human Nature in Politics* (1929), p. 195.
[5] *Ibid.*, p. 187.
[6] Hobhouse, *Development and Purpose* (1913), p. 369.

vacuum. It operates only in relation to experience. To understand this is to see that there is no necessary incompatibility between it and Hobhouses's 'principle of mutuality'. The vital point is, however, that it also is not a blind or automatic impulse, a reflex of the external world, but that it has a determinate nature of its own. Mental activity has to deal with the material to hand; it has to recognize the rest of the facts around it; it operates within a body having varying impulses and needs which is subject to the limitations of its own capacities and those imposed by the world about it; it is a part of that body in operation, a function of that physical entity deriving experience only through it, therefore dependent upon it, existing only with it, and separated by it from all other entities. It is, therefore, distinct and individual, completely alone even as it is at the same time bound up with all the animate and inanimate nature surrounding it. Thus mental activity or the reason is an element of an individual body, an impulse within it to secure harmony of its conceptions, being limited by its nature to the evaluation of its own experience and the integration of its activity in harmony therewith.

Now the harmony thus aimed at is not just any combination, nor yet even a universal of uniform character. It is one that represents an idea of good generated as part of the mental activity of the entity concerned and applied in the sum total of activities of the same entity. That idea is of course not necessarily perfect nor its application complete. It is not a static one, but changes with experience, adapting itself to the facts learnt gradually about the incompatibility of some impulse-satisfactions, the condition of enhancement of some, the limitations imposed by nature and by the external world upon all, and the more recondite possibilities of sublimation. The process of learning can only be by direct experience or by 'inter-learning', that is the assimilation of the observed experience of others until it becomes a part of personal experience. In the measure first, that experience is welded into a consistent idea of good, in measure—that is to say—that it is consistent with itself and with the facts around it, and secondly, that it is acted upon and life lived in harmony with it, will there be self-realization or happiness.

This, which is substantially Hobhouse's concept of harmony,

is also Green's of a moral life when he writes: 'The condition of a moral life is the possession of will and reason. Will is the capacity in a man of being determined to action by the idea of a possible satisfaction of himself. An act of will is an action so determined. . . . Practical reason is the capacity in a man of conceiving the perfection of his nature as an object to be attained by action. All moral ideas have their origin in reason, i.e. in the idea of a possible self-perfection to be attained by the moral agent. This does not mean that the moral agent in every stage of his progress could state this idea to himself in an abstract form.'[1]

Thus to lay self-realization upon the twin foundations of reason and will, or an idea of good and its practical application, is not to claim a universal character for the one, however, or any necessary uniformity for the other. Such an analysis of self-realization does not make it depend upon conformity to an ideal good or a universal reason, nor is the harmony it envisages, which permits the maximum satisfaction of all desires, a formula to be imposed. Rather does it imply the development as a part of each individual separateness of a rational activity which, directed upon the total of experience, issues in what may be called a *weltanschauung* or practical philosophy of life, and the integration of behaviour in harmony with it.

This is not to fall into the palpable error of making excessive claims about human rationality. We can admit with, and learn from, Freud and Marx, for instance, much about the obstacles within our own nature and that of human societies in general to the achievement of rational direction and social harmony. But such lessons of the study of man, his environment, and his history do not establish laws to which he is subject, except in the same sense as, say, laws of physics. The law of gravity does not prevent men from flying. Such further knowledge as they give him are parts of his equipment for intelligently moulding himself and his environment to the realization of his plans. Social determinism, with its emphasis on the environmental, irrational, and subconscious forces which encompass him, often standing in the way of intelligent and purposive direction, is a corrective to false optimism, or fatalistic pessimism, not a proof that he is necessarily the plaything of blind forces. For

[1] *Works*, Vol. II, p. 337.

our knowledge of these does not mean that we cannot interfere, or knowing them control them, though their strength or complexity admittedly encourages some to exchange a determinist pessimism for the over-facile optimism of the earlier rationalists.

It is important at this stage to indicate that the term 'reason' is here being employed to designate that mental activity which is designed to bring order into perceptions. Thus it is empirical, being tied to experience and involving interpretation of experience. Consequently it is something tied to the self, however much it aims at producing generality by comprehending all experience of all selves. Here is where the ambiguity attaches to it. For there is on the other hand the idea of 'pure reason' as a reality existing of its own right regardless of our knowing of it, but which it is the faculty of our reason to know, a theoretic objectivity expressing a universal essence or unity, and thus giving generality to separate individual mental activity and determining its validity. Or, to put it another way, it is not that perfect thing which, as G. Ryle points out, some moralists pretend exists, saying 'My Reason is, what I myself am not yet, perfectly rational'.[1] Rather is it that imperfect thing, so distrusted by the idealist school of political theory because it is limited by my limited nature, which I am aware of in myself and which, despite their strictures, I must use as my best available guide.

This is the same contrast as that drawn by Dewey[2] when he says that 'the new scientific development effects an exchange of reason for intelligence. . . . "Reason" designates both an inherent immutable order of nature, superempirical in character, and the organ of mind by which this universal order is grasped. In both respects, reason is with respect to changing things the ultimate fixed standard—the law physical phenomena obey, the norm human action should obey. For the marks of "reason" in its traditional sense are necessity, universality, superiority to change, domination of the occurrence and the understanding of change.

'Intelligence on the other hand is associated with *judgment*; that is, with selection and arrangement of means to effect consequences and with choice of what we take as our ends. A

[1] *The Concept of Mind* (1949), p. 315.
[2] *Quest for Certainty*, p. 203.

F

man is intelligent not in virtue of having reason which grasps first and indemonstrable truths about fixed principles, in order to reason deductively from them to the particulars which they govern, but in virtue of his capacity to estimate the possibilities of a situation and to act in accordance with his estimate.'

Now it is the second of these concepts that corresponds to the use here of 'reason', the capacity to estimate a situation. But at the same time it must be remembered that each such situation is an aspect of a total situation which is the universe, each such moment estimated a point in history, each such definitive event defined a fleeting fixity in a process of perpetual change. It thus must aim to incorporate that widest nature of understanding which involves generalities or universals.

Reason is thus that process of scientific thought of which W. K. Clifford wrote that 'the truth which it arrives at is not that which we can ideally contemplate without error, but that which we may act upon without fear'.[1] Never should it be forgotten how completely it is tied to the limitations of our thinking and how much the product of our own nature. It is not the reason in 'the technical meaning given to it in classic philosophic tradition' of an inherent and immutable geometry. Rather is it built upon a recognition of the essential part played by man himself in the process of knowing, upon that empirical approach which enabled Clifford to show the inadequacy of the postulates of Euclidean geometry and so to prepare the way for the development of relativity in physics.[2] Man is limited by his own experience and what he can learn from the experience of others, and reason is his attempt to give an orderly interpretation of nature, as he finds it in himself and in his environment. He weaves his estimate of the total situation into a pattern which will involve the making of appraisals. That is his

---

[1] In 'Aims and Instruments of Scientific Thought'.
[2] Chapter 'On the Bending of Space' in *The Commonsense of the Exact Sciences*, by W. K. Clifford (1946), p. 195. 'This assumption (of the worm enclosed in a circular cylinder) is precisely akin to the one we make when we assert that the postulates of Euclidean geometry, which, experience teaches us, are practically true for the space immediately about us, are also true for all space; we assume the sameness of our three-dimensional space. The worm would, however, have better reason for its postulate than we have, because it would have visited every part of its own one-dimensional space. The worm would readily postulate the finiteness of space.'

philosophy or *weltanschauung*, its claim to authority resting not on generalities that can be proved but on its capacity for giving order and meaning to experience, and its claim therefore to have 'good reasons' for it.

For our purposes here what is important is that he looks both inward at his own needs and outward at the conditions of satisfying them. It is true that there are many parts of a man's nature which need satisfying. Some of these needs are more elemental than others—food, shelter, sex, for instance. But even with these there is immense variety in the ways of meeting them, and the capacity of an object to do so is relative not only to its own nature or composition, but to what goes on in the mind of the person with the need which requires satisfying. Food is not only so much protein, calory, or vitamin. Man's body may require certain minimum quantities of each in order to survive in health, but not only do the combinations most suited to different ones vary profoundly, but variations of taste due to conscious preference connected with the mental associations of experience or imagination, or with habit, may vitally affect their actual nutritive value. If it is literally true that one man's food may be another man's poison owing to variations of mental activity and physical construction, how much more is it likely to be true of those elements of human nature which are more complex and diversified than the need for food.

Even in regard to shelter, while the member of a 'civilized' community may perish from exposure when accorded no more than the vagabond's wish for the heaven above and the road below him, the nomad may suffer physical breakdown in the dwelling conditions of a modern industrial city.

The elemental need of sex, psychology reveals as a matter of great complexity in its manifestation, and anthropology shows to lead to an extreme variety of practice and institution. 'It was formerly taken for granted that there existed a certain standard pattern of sexual desire and behaviour and that people whose sexuality did not conform to this accepted pattern must be regarded as abnormal. Most writers on the subject did not bother to describe exactly what the standard pattern was. It was assumed that one knew about it instinctively. At one time it was even believed that those who strayed from the normal standard of sexual behaviour did so deliberately and viciously, but this idea was, to a considerable extent, dispelled. . . .'[1]

Since the work of Freud, Havelock Ellis and their successors such an idea can only appear naïve and inadequate, although it remains the chief ground of law and social attitude on the subject. It is significant that this is particularly true of social systems which have been more influenced by religious authoritarianism than by scientific humanism. For one of the most important lessons of this work—indeed almost its constant refrain—is the connection between failure to reach a self-fulfilling pattern of behaviour for satisfying this part of a man's nature and the fears and repressions engendered in him by authority claiming rightness for a standard pattern, and teaching him to condemn and fear his own spontaneity. 'An arbitrary standard of "good" behaviour originally imposed from without by the threat of punishment has been taken over by a frightened individual and has become the ground of his self-approval. What is hated, despised, disowned, or condemned is his spontaneity: that in himself which, if it were allowed to rise to expression, would expose him again to the "wrath of the Gods". The fear of authority is kept at bay by a continuing act of self-conquest or self-punishment. But the price of peace is the loss of self-possession, for what has been surrendered is the will-to-freedom and what has been substituted is the will-to-obey. This act of making the demands of a feared authority one's own demands upon oneself is repression. It is the result of a moral judgment in which the categorical imperative is external. It is a repudiation of personal responsibility for decision and action. "The good" is thus defined as what we are told to do or to become, and "evil" as anything we want to do or to become that does not coincide.'[2]

The positive lesson is that the liberation of impulse depends upon its conscious recognition, and that realization of the self can be based only on such liberation, followed by the rational determination by the self of a pattern of behaviour in which it will secure fulfilment. Impulse or desire which is not consciously recognized becomes a repression and festers into a neurosis warping the development of the personality and preventing its harmonious fulfilment. For personal responsibility

[1] K. Walker and P. Fletcher, *Sex and Society* (1955), p. 202.
[2] *Ibid.*, p. 147.

is the condition of self-realization. 'When we make a decision freely, on our own responsibility, there is no repression. We have "cut off" one of two open alternatives on our own initiative, knowing in the fullest personal sense what we are doing. Since this "cutting off" is a voluntary withdrawal of interest and attention from the rejected alternative we cease to desire it, and since we are not acting under coercion, none of our energies is consumed in resistance to movement in the direction we have elected to take. Action thus initiated is fruitful and enriching irrespective of whether it is attended by success or failure because it is "wholehearted" or "single-minded": a true personal action and not a "reaction" to coercion. It increases self-possession and self-respect, whereas actions performed under duress invariably have the opposite effect.'[1]

The consequence of such analysis is to show that needs, even elemental physical ones, have to be understood in terms of valuations special to the individual mentality. They are not separable from personality as though they were objective generalized forces to which men react, and which they must express, in predetermined ways. Always they are affected by what goes on in the mind. Indeed it would be nearer to the truth to say that they are given reality only in this way. The idea of a simple physical impulse is utterly inadequate. Fulfilment is attained in a pattern where mental, emotional and physical satisfactions are interrelated as a single harmony but one which may take a great diversity of forms. For example, 'The sex urge becomes one of many manifestations of the creative impulse'.[2] The sensational aspect of impulse satisfaction may be transformed as experience develops the culture of the mind. What is at first a pure impulse satisfaction ceases to be one save insofar as it expresses an idea, and there is an increasing concentration on a more or less conscious pattern of the desirable, to which all sensational aspects may be restricted. They may even disappear altogether in a process of sublimation. In that there is thus a conception of the desirable and a conformity of conduct with it, this subject affords an interesting example in application of a fundamental fact about self-realization. For what is here seen to be taking place is the

[1] *Sex and Society*, p. 147–8.
[2] *Ibid.*, p. 69.

development as a matter of personal responsibility of what we have called a philosophy of life as a preliminary to a rational course of living—in accordance with it.

Such argument from modern psychology resembles Spinoza: 'We cannot be other than what we are, and our whole duty and wisdom is to understand fully our own position in Nature and the causes of our imperfections, and, having understood, to acquiesce; man's greatest happiness and peace of mind (*acquiescentia animi*) comes only from this full philosophical understanding of himself.'[1] Such understanding of himself has to take place, of course, in the perspective of his environment. It is strictly relative. He cannot understand himself in a vacuum but only, as Green said, in relation to other people and things. Indeed his environment is no less than the universe of experience and the more of it his understanding comprehends within its grasp and fits into his philosophy of life the greater will be both his capacity for self-realization and his potentiality of happiness. That 'peace which passeth understanding' is above all the result of a settled, comprehensive, satisfying view of the order of things and his place in it, which integrates his way of life by relation to the single pattern of purpose that it produces. But this pattern must be a matter of personal responsibility truly generated by the self. While it is true that happiness comes from this harmony between will or performance and reason, it is also true that each element of his experience that a man omits from his philosophy reduces its value as a guide, diminishing his capacity for happiness. Less of himself is capable of being fulfilled. The greater is the possibility of a discordant factor in his way of life leaving him dissatisfied. If some inhibition on the working of his reason causes him to seek 'escape from freedom' by way of refusing to face some fact of his nature—of potential pleasure or of necessary limitation—he reduces the compass of his fulfilment and will sooner or later find that his life is out of harmony with his experience. Such disharmony may result either because his purpose does not comprehend it or because his behaviour does not conform to it. And it is such disharmony which is the obverse of self-realization.

This is to say, with Hobhouse, that all parts of a man's nature must be satisfied, insofar as they are capable of harmonization,

[1] Stuart Hampshire, *Spinoza*, p. 121.

if he is to achieve that harmony of satisfaction which is self-fulfilment. But it is also to stress the role played by reason or intelligence in this process as the means by which alone he can recognize all parts of his nature and mould them into a whole which accords with his philosophy of life. And this, it must be emphasized, may lead him to derive no happiness from satisfying some impulse or part of his nature, to withdraw interest or desire from it. For this means that it is the refusal to recognize the impulse not the refusal to satisfy it that produces the disharmony.

For it is important not to make the mistake of thinking in static terms. That man is in a continuous state of becoming is implicit in the very idea of purpose. The parts of his nature, his impulses or desires, are not fixed elements unaffected by his mental activities. On the contrary, while it is true that they often influence the working of the mind, this in its turn gives direction and meaning to them, strengthening some, weakening others, until we reach a point where there is no paradox in saying that some physical pain may give him mental pleasure or some physical pleasure give him mental pain. And at that stage each has lost its initial significance: the former has become a satisfaction, the latter a dissatisfaction. One need has replaced another; one has atrophied, another grown; all as the result of processes in which mental activity has taken a leading part, whether by the association of ideas, through imagination, by conscious reasoning, or by 'learning from experience', in this development of purpose. And the picture of a man as one complex of needs has ceased to be true; he has become another.

Now, the universe of experience thus integrated by the reason into what we have called a philosophy of life, or *weltanschauung*, includes, of course, all the facts of man's sociality. Although there is an inescapable element of separateness in every man, he is no Robinson Crusoe, but by nature and necessity a member of social groups. Both his need of others and their need of him are an inevitable part of his experience. He can no more disregard or blind himself to this than to the other physical facts of his nature and environment. He has to learn what he wants and the conditions on which he can get it. He has to discover too what others expect of him and what are the pleasures and pains associated with satisfying or disappointing their expectations. The process is an individual one in that he alone can interpret and integrate into a meaningful pattern his own experience. And in this sense the individualist political thinkers are right. But the process is also one in which society plays an important role. A major part of his experience arises out of the fact of his belonging to social groups all through his life. From the moment of his birth he is submitted to the influence of others: he imitates them, is taught by them, learns from their experience, behaviour, and ideas; he enters into a whole social tradition that he inherits from the past; he reacts to the place and conditions of society in which he finds himself.

But this analysis of self-realization entails the recognition that the danger is much less that his uniqueness shall issue in eccentricity or dissidence, perilous to society but having meaning for himself, than that it shall be subjected to a stereotype unrelated to his own experience, which is never therefore rationally integrated by him, does not produce a sense of direction in him, and leaves him rudderless and frustrated. The objective of finding and pursuing the good life is thus lost in an uncharted sea of social habit, convention, and meaningless conformity, and political purpose is unachieved.

For the notion that political purpose can be realized in obedience to such a stereotype worked out and commanded by authority is a fundamentally false one. Not only does it lead to frustration in the citizen; but it is self-defeating from the point of view of society, which can never produce the sense of community, and the active promotion of common ends, unless these are grounded in rational acceptance of them by its members. The slave is a less productive worker than the free man, the mercenary a less effective soldier than the armed citizen fighting for his own city. It is the consciousness of shared purposes, of being needed for the common endeavour, and of participation in creative activity which not only gave to many in wartime the sense of an integrated life and personal fulfilment but made possible an exceptionally high order of collective achievement. Danger of course may spur on to unusual effort but there was more in it than this, for even when there was no keen sense of personal danger a heightened meaning was given to activity by the awareness of its serving purposes jointly accepted, and the result was both exceptional social cohesion and exceptional social achievement.

There are significant institutional consequences of such analysis of reason and political purpose. Emphasis is laid by it on the importance of the conscious development of rationally determined concepts of purpose. It gives special weight to freedom of discussion as the means necessary to the defining of such concepts and to the arrival at agreement upon them. Their open consideration, untrammelled by preconceptions and prohibitions, and the willingness to submit them to the test of experience, is most likely to make them satisfactory practical ideals. For them to be satisfactory they must satisfy the demands of experience. This means that each must contribute the report of his own, since there is an element in it which is individual or unique. Similarity of experience is most likely to lead to agreement but there can be no absolute certainty of agreement, and the most we can do is to encourage the exchange of report, that is the communication of ideas. But the judgment or appraisal is made by the individual intelligence and where it differs the most we can do is to aim at reasonably satisfactory compromise. This is to stress the essential primacy of education, and a particular kind of education aimed above all at the promotion of personal responsibility, as well as the free pursuit of knowledge. It is to give preference to systems of persuasion over those of command. It is to encourage the recognition of personality rather than conformity, respecting character more than social function, defining social or political purpose as common purpose, that is agreement between personal appraisals. And it is to see in such unity of appraisal or sharing of purpose the foundation of that co-operative association which is the state, and whose institutions must reflect this process. The institutional consequences are thus the recognition of the need to promote the conscious sharing in purposes which the intelligence or reason freely accepts. Creative activity follows only from such acceptance. Institutions must therefore embody it and facilitate concordant activity. Self-realization, or fulfilment of personality, requiring that life be lived in accordance with a practical philosophy of life or planned design for living, which expresses an attempt at a rational harmonization of needs and desires, it follows that law and social policy can be valued according to its capacity to evoke in the members of society active acceptance. Inasmuch as it applies their *weltan-*

schauung will obedience to it be fulfilling. But this is not a case of the general will constraining men to be free, for the act of acceptance, in order to be thus creative, must in each case be an act of conscious decision or be capable of being so.

This is why it is a mistake, in an endeavour to avoid what is deprecatingly called 'atomistic' individualism, to imagine that the uniqueness of each individual can be safely forgotten or merged into averages, and that only 'social' facts or the workings of masses socially organized require consideration. The truth is that man is not an automaton of whom all it is necessary to know is the content of his environment because he will reflect it as effect follows cause. There is always in his behaviour an element of free choice. We do in fact invariably talk and act on the assumption of this. If we did not it would become meaningless to praise or blame. Just as we may condemn ourselves, regret some deed, suffer remorse for it, resolve to act otherwise in future, which we could not do if we could not have acted differently, so are we entitled to praise or blame the behaviour of another or of a society.

The over-stressing of environment may be the natural result of past under-emphasis but reaction from an excessive emphasis on his individuality, placed in direct antithesis to society—Spencer's 'Man versus the State'—has gone too far when it treats him as though he were, not it is true any longer the slave of an ordained ruler or the creature of an authoritarian state, but the inevitable outcome of a process of purely social causation, and the creation of ordered society. The most that can be said is that society plays a highly significant part in his development and that social studies give guidance and suggest probabilities. We have always also to accept the uniqueness of experience and its variation from one subject to another, the fact that experience can only be, as it were, focused in the rational processes of the individual mind.

Environment and social conditions are, of course, of the greatest importance but they are not everything. Their impact on the individual is not precisely knowable in all its effects. Both he and they are too complex and no two individuals can be safely assumed to be exactly the same. We are in fact unable to predict as we should expect to be able to do, were it possible to show human behaviour as an inevitable reaction to known external causes or given social conditions. Yet there are certainly elements of regularity and predictability, as statistical analysis of group attitudes amply serves to show. If we want to predict, for instance, what political party and policy a country will favour, to know all the facts of the situation will probably give us a quite inadequate basis for prediction. On the other hand once we know the decision actually taken by a sample group, as in a by-election or a Gallup poll, we find from experience that other groups, and the electorate as a whole, may be expected to make much the same judgment. This suggests that although we do not know in advance from a knowledge of the situation what form the judgment on it will take, once we have learnt what it is in one group of cases, we can reasonably expect it to be broadly the same in a similar group of cases. Thus it is true that we do find uniformities, or, what amounts to the same thing, a regularity in the variations of reaction. But these result from a number of individual appraisals and are not a substitute for them. This is important because, unless we realize that we are reporting a consensus of wills determined by a series of acts of free choice, we may suggest a determinism implying the absence of acts of decision. We are depicting agreement, not predestination. But what is meant by determinism is the absence of choice. Because choice can often be predicted it is inferred that it does not take place. To quarrel with this is not to question that choice can be explained, or even that it can frequently be anticipated.

We can, indeed, without resorting to a false determinism, suggest causal connections in the behaviour of societies. We can even suggest probabilities that may help us to predict social reactions to given sets of circumstances. And this would not be so if behaviour were wholly unaccountable. Its regularities and uniformities do make it, provided these conditions are remembered, a subject suitable for scientific analysis. Reasonably convincing explanations of the course of social change can be offered. To offer them is a legitimate enterprise, whether it be Gibbon or Montesquieu explaining the decline of Rome, Carlyle tracing the influence of great men, or Marx the impact on the political system of changes in the organization of production. What is not legitimate is to claim that such analysis can establish laws with which societies must or ought to conform or rules of historical inevitability.

VI

THE INDIVIDUAL AND MORALITY

(a) Morality: not a Self-evident Absolute

THE emphasis on agreement as opposed to predestination has constantly recurred. Of the recognition of authority and the obligation to obey we have said that it springs from a unity of purpose and shared ideals. We have seen purpose as necessarily related to judgment, and political purpose as an attempt at such a rational combination of these judgments that it will evoke general and actively conscious acceptance. Social ends we have sought to show as reflecting a consensus of wills. Of the value of the state we have claimed that it is always a relative value, relative, that is, to the evaluation of its acts by reference to their success in fulfilling the purposes of its citizens. Though that is not of course to claim any finality for such evaluation, or to deny that other evaluations may be made, it does express an attempt at finality since to value is by definition to apply standards which satisfy the reason, and this they can only do, if they appear the best ones available.

Now the common characteristic of these propositions is that they all invoke a reference to judgment exercised by a more or less specific group of human beings. They have an element of relativity; they do not imply that there will be any ultimate perfection in the actual conclusions which emerge from them. Thus they are in contrast with the idea of purpose or value as existing of its own right because it expresses some super-empirical reality which imposes itself, a self-evident first principle by which every judgment can itself be judged.

This contrast between ideals created by intelligent activity, or social purpose produced by co-operation, and a stereotype moulding to a predetermined pattern of perfection has its counterpart in the discussion of morality. For here, in particular strength, do we find the notion of an absolute or objective body of principles existing of their own right, which we automatically perceive—'thou shalt not kill; thou shalt not commit adultery' —whose truth we grasp by intuition, and which it is our duty to obey. It is in opposition to this notion that we see morality as an empirical, tentative pattern of beliefs, the common denominator of a myriad of personal moral ideals, each tested by the ends of intelligent activity and shared purpose.

On the one hand, and to an extent of which we are not always aware, social and political speculation of modern times has tended to treat man as part of a mechanical universe, in which he is subject to 'moral laws' judged to be as much a part of that universe as the 'laws' of physics. It has assumed the existence of a purpose in the universe, which is expressed in moral rules. Morality therefore reflects this purpose within the universe which is entirely distinct from the purposes of men themselves. As Collingwood has pointed out, a similarly anthropomorphic approach to history has treated succeeding events as the unfolding of thoughts in a universal mind, and not as the expression of thoughts in the minds of those who make events. Both errors alike arise from an unproved metaphysical assumption, and flourish in an atmosphere largely created by biological theories of evolution.

On the other hand, an inductive study of morality shows that there are as many moralities as there are societies. We can examine social morality comparatively, taking examples from what we find in the Trobriand Islands, in Islam, in Nazi Germany, Japan, in Communist Russia, or in contemporary England. The belief that there are moral values which all men accept at all times as self-evident and for which it is senseless to demand reasons, or which excite immediate and universal emotions of approval, and that therefore there is a morality, 'objective' in the sense that it is stored up somewhere in imperishable form beyond the reach of argument or the test of experience, is akin to the idea that everyone is endowed with a conscience, which is an infallible instrument for separating right from wrong. But neither corresponds to the facts. There is no such certainty, and we just simply do not always know. That is not of course to say that we are not often agreed on an important body of moral principles. There is no doubt a nucleus of these which grows and which no one of this generation and in this society would deny. But they are not self-evident; rather are they the embodiment of arrangements that have been tested and found to provide satisfactory conditions of life, which their absence would remove or undermine.[1] Empirical, they are thus the result of applying intelligence to experience.

Such an insistence on the empirical in morality may seem to be an endorsement of ethical relativity, but it is not. There is plenty of evidence of the different forms which common moral judgments and agreed evaluations take. Westermarck emphasizes them. But there is also plenty of evidence of similarity. Ginsberg stresses this, and Westermarck himself admits that 'when we study the moral rules laid down by the customs of savage peoples we find that they in a very large measure resemble the rules of civilized nations'. We can safely assert of many principles that nearly everyone would accept them. Surely however there is truth in both views. The fact of change and difference reminds us of their subjective empirical basis and their incompleteness; that of their similarity points to the stability they represent, and this suggests a tendency to real objectivity in them. There is wide agreement, as Ginsberg points out, on such duties as those of fidelity, reparation, requital, equitable distribution, beneficence, and non-maleficence or non-injury.[2] Comparative study reveals much uniformity of moral judgments.

When considering the possibility of discovering foundations for political theory we encountered the view that these are unnecessary because moral criteria are already to hand in the society about us. It was here implied that we do not need to go beyond them, or even perhaps that we cannot. But this is surely not true. We do in fact want to seek beyond such criteria for the reasons for them. To do this we must compare them with alternatives. By this means alone can we provide for their strengthening, and for that development which undoubtedly takes place in moral ideas. Refusal to accept as adequate 'the

---

[1] See below, pp. 119, and following for further discussion of this.
[2] M. Ginsberg, *Reason and Unreason in Society* (1947), p. 25.

criteria to hand' is to reject ethical relativism. Incest, human sacrifice, slavery, public hanging, the death penalty for minor offences against property, or for reasons of political or religious opinion, or even for belonging to a particular race, have all come within the criteria accepted by societies of which we have record, and most of them in very recent times. Yet we want to know why we reject them and why we regard their rejection as preferable to their acceptance. But had we lived in any of the societies which accepted them, and at the same time regarded morality as an 'objective', self-evident body of principles, we should in all probability have accepted them too.

For we cannot escape the dilemma. Either morality is absolute, being something ordained by an authority beyond man. It can then be regarded as 'objective' in the sense that it is a preordained part of a universal order, a system like the physical universe working in accordance with fixed rules, and without regard to human purposes. These rules, moreover, are knowable; they can be recognized by anyone who takes the trouble to study them; they thus become a firmly established body of truth accepted—whether through the operation of emotion, conscience, or reason—by all. This particular physical analogy has greatly influenced moral speculation. This is so although modern physics seems to throw increasing doubt on the fixity of its rules, which, in any case, are not 'laws' to be 'obeyed' but observational generalizations whose truth is subject to empirical test, that from time to time requires their modification, and seems now to have converted a machine-like universe into an expanding one. The significance of the analogy with the physical universe, regarded as representing a determinate, objective and predictable order, is that it suggests the existence of an autonomous moral order created by a force or authority beyond man, just as is the universe itself. Thus it is something which, once discovered—whether by church, state, or even positivist academy—is absolute and has the supreme claim to enforcement.

Or morality, on the other hand, is something which expresses human purposes. In that case it must be subjective in the sense that it is derived from the judgment of good made by men out of their own experience, and if we want to claim any objectivity for it this must rely upon the extent to which judgments agree and can be shown in a coherent system, and be limited always at the point where coherence or agreement is not forthcoming. Social morality regarded as the commonly accepted standard of a society in this case is derivative and subordinate, and always subject to emendation. Its foundation lies in the coincidence of personal moral ideals. There are ways, it is true, in which we can seek to make it appear more objective and less relative, and that in itself may win it acceptance. These ways are the search first for common elements in human purpose, and then for common guides to their practical achievement in society. This leads us, we have suggested, to seek some guidance in the analysis of such concepts as self-realization, happiness, the good life, because they help in the definition of human purpose. To consider too in what conditions and by what means these ends can be most fully reached in turn leads us to test systems or institutions of co-operation, such as the state itself, by the criterion of the expression and achievement of common ends. But we must never forget if we use objectivity in this way that the only test to which, in the last resort, an objective moral principle can be submitted must include an element of individual preference. This approach to morality does not deny the possibility that there may be a moral order in the universe; on that subject it retains an open mind, only asserting that we have no means of establishing what it is.

As it is argued here that we cannot adopt the first alternative because we cannot find the universal acceptance of a single body of moral truth which it postulates, although we may think we are moving towards it, we must examine more fully the nature and consequence of the second. And we cannot do better than begin with Westermarck's analysis.

Although Westermarck finds the source of moral judgment in the emotions of approval and disapproval, he asserts that these emotions are modified by thought, indeed that the more they are so the more advanced is the morality in which they result. This can only mean that they are subjected to and guided by a reasoning process. The explanation of his emphasis on emotion rather than reason appears to lie in his fear that the admission of a rational guide will lead to the acceptance of a 'super-empirical order of nature' as the basis of moral judgments; for this he regards not only as a chimera, but as a dangerous opening to further fallacies. Since, according to him, moral concepts have an emotional origin they must spring from what is within experience and therefore be subjective. They may be discussed —and with more profit than, for instance, beauty—but 'there are points in which unanimity cannot be reached even by the most accurate presentation of the facts or the subtlest process of reasoning.'[1] He denies the existence of an ultimate standard of objectivity—such as Bentham's utilitarianism or Spencer's 'that which conduces to life in each and all'—saying that there is always a point at which the most rational cannot agree.

Nevertheless he admits that there is moral progress, which means that we can compare moral judgments, or 'the moral law' at one time and another, and claim that one is better—or more moral—than another. 'We shall find,' he says, 'that the evolution of the moral consciousness to a large extent consists in its development from the unreflecting to the reflecting.'[2] We shall return to this implicit criterion of morality; it gives valuable support to our central argument. But it is important first to consider the explanation given by Westermarck of the widespread acceptance of the view that morality has the quality of an objective certainty.

Morality is currently taken to connote behaviour having social approval, behaviour which we have learnt to call good by custom, by the teaching of parents, of school, friends, religion. 'Particular modes of conduct have their traditional labels, many of which are learnt with language itself.'[3] 'The emotional origin of all moral concepts,'[4] however, explains why 'it may be fairly doubted whether the same mode of conduct ever arouses exactly the same degree of indignation or approval in any two individuals.'

We are tempted to ascribe to it a degree of objectivity it lacks by two facts. The first is 'the relative uniformity of moral opinions'. But this, nevertheless, is very much dissolved by any extended examination of what are held, or have been held, as moral opinions. This reveals their great variation. Westermarck's work is quite sufficient to prove this. Such extended

---
[1] *The Origin and Development of the Moral Ideas*, Vol. I, p. 11.
[2] *Ibid.*, Vol. I, p. 10.
[3] *Ibid.*, Vol. I, p. 9.
[4] *Ibid.*, Vol. I, p. 13.

examination, however, is not undertaken by the ordinary person. He is indeed always only too ready to accept the actual as the natural and inevitable. And the fact of the considerable uniformity of opinions prevailing in the society to which he belongs,[1] owing though it so largely is to common teaching, custom, tradition, prejudice, encourages him to believe that the moral law is something existing outside himself, the proof of its existence lying in what he thinks is its universal acceptance, and not something deriving its authority from his, and his fellows', scales of preference—that is from its evocation in him and others of sentiments or judgments of approval or condemnation.

The second is 'the authority which, rightly or wrongly, is ascribed to moral rules. From our earliest childhood we are taught that certain acts *are* right and that others *are* wrong. Owing to their exceptional importance for human welfare, the facts of the moral consciousness are emphasized in a much higher degree than any other subjective facts. We are allowed to have our private opinions about the beauty of things, but we are not so readily allowed to have our private opinions about right and wrong. The moral rules which are prevalent in the society to which we belong are supported by appeals not only to human, but to divine, authority, and to call in question their validity is to rebel against religion as well as against public opinion. Thus the belief in a moral order of the world has taken hardly less firm hold of the human mind, than the belief in a natural order of things. And the moral law has retained its authoritativeness even when the appeal to an external authority has been regarded as inadequate. It filled Kant with the same awe as the star-spangled firmament. According to Butler, conscience is "a faculty in kind and in nature supreme over all others, and which bears its own authority of being so". Its supremacy is said to be "felt and tacitly acknowledged by the worst no less than by the best of men". Adam Smith calls the moral faculties the "viceregents of God within us".' In measure, however, that agreement about them is lacking, there can be no certainty as to what they are, whatever may be the strength of the opinion that they should be obeyed.

Social morality, then, being a compound of individual

---

[1] It is only fair to add, as we have already noted, that Westermarck also finds an even wider similarity in moral judgments. See his *Ethical Relativity*, p. 196.

moralities, although these are of course greatly influenced by what society teaches and seeks to impose, ideas of it are found to vary with the time and place in which it is generated. The grounds on which it can claim observance, therefore, are not self-evident or absolute. A code of behaviour which produces a response of approval in one society or one individual at one time may produce a response of indignation at another: it is in conformity with social or individual morality in the former but not in the latter case. It is dependent on what is thought to be a satisfactory way of living together, and that in turn upon what is found in practice to satisfy. Thus it is the product of thought and experience, and not of an *a priori* relationship with nature, evolution, the divine order, or law of historical development. The answer, that is to say, is likely to be plural and therefore controversial, rather than monistic and therefore properly enforced by the strongest sanctions.

But the lack of objective certainty, for which the work of Westermarck and others gives abundant evidence, does not imply the impossibility of rational criteria of moral concepts which is sometimes inferred. We are now much readier to admit the subjective limitations to the rational process.[1] Outside textbook definitions there is no necessary opposition between the subjective and the rational; nor in real life is there a complete synonymity between the objective truth and the rational structure which is assumed to establish it. The same doubt exists about the final validity of what is deemed objective reason at any given moment as about an objective morality. To study the history of political thought is to become aware that what is accepted as a rational manner of argument can change from one period to another. What are good reasons for one century are not always so for a later one. Conclusions drawn from analogy which would satisfy a mediaeval scholar carry no conviction to one of today. Many ways of thinking have been discarded and, we believe, rightly so. To admit this is not to throw doubt on improvement. It is not to question that our good reasons are better ones than those once acceptable. Nor is it to dispute the necessity for acting on the best available. But it should discourage arrogance. If our reasoning process is better

[1] Cf. for instance, Michael Polanyi, 'On the Introduction of Science into Moral Subjects,' *Cambridge Journal*, Vol. VII, p. 4.

it is unlikely to have reached perfection. But this does not involve the denial of reason as a criterion of moral concepts. In their evolution Westermarck himself sees an increasing element of reflection, which is to say that they are more and more submitted to rational tests, and that the more they are so the better are they likely to be.

What are these tests? While it may not be possible to discover some simple, final, and all-inclusive first principle—such as Bentham, Herbert Spencer and others have believed in—it certainly is often possible to find a wide agreement in the preference of one moral concept to another, and invariably to relate the preference to the belief on the part of the person concerned that it is more conducive to his happiness or the good life for him or a satisfactory way of living with others. This general or widespread acceptance may not be conclusive, or have attached to it any certainty of final truth, but it does seem to be based on a process of reasoning from experience. The necessary element of doubt as to the validity of its conclusions, while it should induce an attitude of tolerance does not imply the abdication of the rational judgment from control. On the contrary, owing to the importance of moral issues, there is every call for reason to be brought as fully to bear as possible upon them. The emotions are a poor guide indeed without the checks and control of reflection. Men even in their most primitive condition are dimly aware of this for they evidently feel the need to support moral precepts not only by reference to a supernatural authority, which ordains a particular order in human relations, but by alleging harmful consequences of their infraction.

It can also be claimed that in the process of 'development from the unreflecting to the reflecting' there is a constant tendency to accept happiness, immediate or ultimate, as the touchstone assumed, although in its earlier forms this may mean little more than the avoidance of disaster. But the argument is not that there is any universal recognition of the idea that moral rules are directed to happiness, or that such an idea is self-evident, or commends itself spontaneously to everyone approaching any such question. Rather is it that it comes nearer than any other explanation to providing a realistic, orderly and rational guide to developing moral notions.

There is no disproof of such an argument in Westermarck's remark that a Fuegian would not understand if he were told that the principle 'I ought not to prefer my own lesser good to the greater good of another' underlay and explained some such moral rule as not to wreak vengeance by killing. It might well be added that neither would many other people more capable of abstract reasoning than Westermarck's Fuegian. The practice of wreaking vengeance by killing is a highly uncomfortable one for any society; and there can surely be little doubt that insofar as it has disappeared from modern societies this is mainly due to the discovery that the comforts of security are greater than those of the vendetta, that restraint upon the pleasures of revenge or of gratifying vindictiveness by personal violence may be more than compensated by the advantages enjoyed through the existence of laws, courts, and police, and that the principles of reciprocity and equality of claim are a necessary basis of this. The principle of the lesser and greater good is only to be commended, and can only be convincingly commended, on such grounds as these. For, besides wanting my own immediate good, even if a lesser one, what I prefer is also a system of society in which my greater good will take precedence over another's lesser good, and experience teaches me to recognize in this principle an essential term of the co-operation through which this can be secured.

(b) *Morality as Individual Self-realization*

Recognition of the impossibility of discerning metaphysical foundations for morality does not prevent us, however, from finding much that is illuminating in the further reasoning of T. H. Green on the subject of morality, and in particular on the idea of self-realization as central to this. Green's influence on political theory was considerable for at least half a century, and in this particular connection the later doubts on the importance of his contribution are least justified. To say, as we have done, that the morality of action depends on its according with a pattern of purpose which itself fits into a *weltanschauung* or philosophy of life, is not altogether to differ from Green's view that acts must be 'done for the sake of their goodness, and not for the sake of any pleasure or any satisfaction of desire which they bring to the agent'. Rather is it to say that they must do both, and that Green's is in some degree an unreal alternative. For it is clear that activity will be more fully satisfying to us—which is another way of saying that we will derive more pleasure from it—if it is in harmony with our principles of right and proper conduct than if it is in conflict with them. In other words, one of the desires themselves which are contending within us for fulfilment is the desire to do things for the sake of their goodness, or to do only that which we can approve. Inasmuch, indeed, as by goodness we mean that which we approve—regardless, for the moment, of whether others approve it—this desire has the peculiarity that it affects all other desires, for we can satisfy it only to the extent that we are able to approve all the other desires we satisfy. Thus it is a basic desire in the sense that it is one to integrate the others and to be met only through the medium of meeting them; and unless it is met at the same time as they are, and through them, the result of satisfying them is an ambivalence producing conflict rather than content. Thus it would be nearer the truth to modify Green's dictum by saying that unless acts are done for the sake of something which includes a belief in their goodness they cannot satisfy.

Green goes on to say that 'it is impossible that an action should be done for the sake of its goodness unless it has been previously contemplated as good for some other reason than that which consists in its being done for the sake of its goodness. In other words, a prior morality . . . is the condition of there coming to be a character governed by interest in an ideal of goodness.'[1] But this is compatible with the argument here put forward that for action to be moral it must be in harmony with the results of reflection on the nature of good. Pleasure or satisfaction to the agent has a double part to play in this process. First, it is the consequence of action in accordance with his ideal of goodness. Secondly, his ideal of goodness, or his idea of a prior morality, is itself a formulation of a system designed to secure his happiness. And the only test of validity of a philosophy of life, acting in accordance with which will give the fullest satisfaction, is experience, for experience alone can teach whether it does in fact do so.

[1] *Works*, Vol. II, p. 335–6.

We thus do in fact say that it is important to seek the reasons for moral criteria. And it is here that attempts to analyse the good life may contribute reasons, and that concepts such as self-realization may illuminate the enquiry into how moral ideas are formed.

Now, if such a view is not in conflict with Green's claim that a prior morality is implicit in this definition of morality, it does differ both from his and from Hobhouse's assumption that the idea of goodness with which conformity is required derives its authority from the fact that it exists in a 'social mind'. There is a difficulty in Hobhouse's statement, with its metaphysical implications, that 'The "good" is what is accepted, approved or encouraged by someone, not necessarily by self. As soon as the self clearly recognizes its goodness that is tantamount to a practical acceptance. To learn the meaning of the word is to assimilate and fit on to our own feeling ideas that are moving in the social life around us.'[1] For it seems to make it a condition of the good that it shall first be conceived by someone else. And my process of reflection is not one of perceiving, but one of accepting or assimilating from another. While it is perfectly true that we do get our ideas mainly from those that are moving around us, that are in the air of the society in which we find ourselves, the chief importance lies in the fact of acceptance. That acceptance, in any case, is selective: it is not all ideas current in our day which we thus accept. And it is the selection we make that produces our own peculiar combination, and our own individual attitude to life or *weltanschauung*. To argue otherwise is surely to mistake the material of judgment for judgment itself. Moreover, if the selection is not made by man it must be made in some way beyond the will of man; and Hobhouse comes in the end to assume not only 'a certain unity pervading all mind',[2] but also an entity indistinguishable from the comprehensive social self-conscious Being of the idealists; and the consequence is that morality is placed upon a metaphysical foundation.

The theory of morality put forward here[3] relates it instead to the reason and will operating upon circumstance. As Green

[1] *The Rational Good* (1921), p. 92.
[2] *Ibid.*, p. 89.
[3] See especially Chapter V, above.

says, 'Self-satisfaction is for ever sought and found in the realization of a completely articulated or thoroughly filled idea of the perfection of the human person'. This idea each must build out of his own experience. What he requires of it is that it shall interpret his experience. It is true that there are many different parts of his nature, many instinctive and other needs, which demand satisfaction if he is to lead a full life. It is true too that he must achieve a satisfactory integration of himself with the universe external to himself, physical and social, with material conditions, and with other human beings. But this integration, both internal and external, in order to achieve the quality of an 'idea of the perfection of the human person', can only come from an impulse within himself, not within the universe external to himself. Will must accord with this rational impulse, behaviour with this idea, if realization of the self is to be the outcome. That is the essential reconciliation of will and reason which lies at the root of morality. In spite of Green it cannot be equated with subjection of the will to 'conventional morality'. Convenient though it would be to find that such subjection is the equivalent of self-realization, it is so only to the extent that everyone thinks alike. Yet inasmuch as self-realization is a satisfactory way of describing the purpose of men it must be the purpose of society too. There are practical limits, of course, to its achievement set by the conditions of social life. But there are possibilities of misunderstanding in the way that Hobhouse sets forth the proposition: 'self-development is not as such an element in the social ideal, but only such development as contributes to the harmony of the social whole.'[2] For, while we may say that the need for social harmony limits the possibilities of self-development because all self-development may not be compatible, we must add that the greater the extent to which social need permits self-development the more is social purpose achieved. For the end of society is social harmony only as the means for achieving the greatest possible self-realization.

[1] *Works*, Vol. II, p. 329.
[2] *Rational Good*, p. 93.

VII

SOCIALITY
AND MORALITY

NOW it may be said that the approach to the problem so far adopted is one-sided. It has stressed one aspect of the subject: the separateness of the individual, the uniqueness of experience, the unity of the self over against all other selves. And it may be contended that the basis so far provided for defining the judgment of the good life, lying as it does in the individual's valuation, might be used to claim the same moral value for a judgment that issues in an anti-social ideal as for one that induces a life devoted to the disinterested service of mankind. This would be a mistaken view, however, because by nature man is not only an individual but a social creature, who has by force of nature and circumstance to adapt himself to his own social needs. For his moral ideal has to provide for the needs that spring from both these parts of his experience, his social character and the conditions of life in society, from his necessary sociality as well as his individuality. That is the essential duality which neither the individualist, nor the idealist determinist, political theory can escape, but which both often fail to meet.

Because of man's sociality the idea of self-realization as the test of social purpose is open to criticism if it is given a narrow interpretation—based only on his separateness. 'The concept of self-satisfaction, though it serves to emphasize the vitalizing and liberative aspects of ideals, is inadequate because it neglects the elements of obligation and fails to bring out the importance of the larger form or order of life within which the ideals are embedded and which therefore goes beyond the individual.'[1] To avoid this narrow interpretation the personal moral ideal must be seen as springing from the total needs of the self, that is to say in its dual aspect. It is only inadequate if it makes an unreal isolation of the self, taking into consideration only its first aspect, its separateness. But the elements of obligation, it must be repeated, attach to the personal moral ideal which reflects the dual character of the self, as social also. The idea of obligation would itself be inadequate if it dealt only with the larger, social order of life, forgetting that this attains its validity by being included within, or focused in, the personal moral ideal. For obligation is neither to the self nor to others but to an idea which because it is generated by mental activity must be the product of the self, but which because the self is subject to social needs and influences must be inclusive of these also. Once this is recognized it becomes possible to enter upon an analysis of this idea freed from the inconsistency of asserting either that it can exist otherwise than in individual minds, that is in a social mind; or that obligation can lie at the same time in more than one direction—for example, in the conscience and in something called, according to preference, social morality or law and institutions.

Since this idea must be comprehensive of, and integrate, all experience it has been called above a *weltanschauung*, or philosophy of life. It is a moral ideal because it issues in judgment of right and wrong, but it is a philosophy in that it is an attempt to incorporate and interpret total experience and express it in a consistent pattern of living. Thus it would not be possible with this use of the term 'philosophy', to accept the view that 'a satisfactory life does not depend upon philosophical knowledge; indeed, such knowledge is irrelevant to it.'[2] For everything that increases our knowledge of ourselves and of the world we live in may help us in the necessary process of adapting our lives to reality. But it should be added that this may be a special use of the term 'philosophy' as equivalent to Green's term 'practical philosophy' which, though suitable for our purposes here, may not be acceptable to the authorities of the discipline of pure philosophy today. Perhaps it may be fair to say that this is so because we are attempting to build on psychology in the

[1] Ginsberg, *Basic Needs and Moral Ideals*, p. 204.
[2] Oakeshott, *Experience and Its Modes*, p. 339.

tradition of Locke and Hume rather than on logic in that of Bradley, or on the empirical rather than the metaphysical.

This is to contend that the analysis of the nature of man, of the purposes that spring from it, and of the conditions of their achievement in the world as we know it is the only solid subject-matter for discussion of moral ideals. It is to say 'that they are ends which are built up out of the basic needs by a process of constructive imagination, spurred on by disappointments and failures, directly experienced or vividly realized through sympathy with others.'[1] It is thus to place the analysis in the utilitarian tradition with the implication that morality has to do with the satisfaction of the sum-total of needs. That sum comprises quite different and sometimes antagonistic types of need. They could no doubt be classified in many ways, but it will be convenient here to consider them as threefold, those of the body, those of the mind, and those arising from man's need for other human beings. It is with the last that we shall now be mainly concerned. The first two types are obvious. We have already entered into some discussion of them, and we find them frequently made the basis of assertions of 'natural rights'. It is of them that Herbert Spencer is speaking when he bases natural right on the need to preserve life, asserting that man has a natural right to what is essential to that end.[2] Discussing rights in the modern state, Laski gives pride of place to the right to work which he defines in such a way as to include the right to be paid a wage sufficient to cover food, shelter, a certain modicum of additional comfort and of leisure,[3] and goes on to the right to education. Maintenance of bodily health and the free operation of the mind are indeed the patent prerequisites for the achievement of human purpose. They are indisputably basic needs. The state is bound by them. Society having as its aim the good life is presumptively directed to their satisfaction as its most elementary function, as a condition of its very existence. But they are relative to time and place and physical possibility, and raise considerations of a different order from those involved in man's basic social needs.

Analysis of the nature of man shows at once how extensive

[1] Ginsberg, *Basic Needs and Moral Ideals*, p. 201.
[2] *The Man versus the State* (1885), p. 96.
[3] *Grammar of Politics* (1928), p. 107.

is the social aspect of the satisfaction of basic needs. Indeed there are few even of the physical and mental needs which do not involve others. In infancy man is dependant for the supplying of his wants; and the more complex the society in which he grows up the greater is the degree of dependance in which he continues for the rest of his life. The same is true of his mental needs, to understand the world about him, to give play to his imagination. Information and ideas are supplied to him—and the whole working of his mind fundamentally influenced thereby—through parents, teachers, friends, books, works of art. Together with his own observation they provide the material of his rational thought; they affect his interpretation of the world and his formulation of purpose. Though he becomes increasingly selective in his use of such material as this, he never entirely emancipates himself from dependance upon it. He needs to talk, to express his ideas, to share them with others and test them against those of others, to influence others and obtain their agreement.

Social influences even upon the consciousness of basic physical needs are profoundly important. Imitation leads to the discovery of satisfactions which from habits become essentials. Social culture modifies the relative emphasis on needs and may largely determine their form of expression and fulfilment. 'Whereas some theorists suggest that our cultural achievements depend on "sublimating" the tremendous pressure of sex, it is arguable that the tremendous pressure of sex is itself one of our most curious cultural achievements.'[1]

There is thus the social influence on the definition of man's physical and mental needs; but there is also his dependance upon others to meet them, and his direct need for others for themselves. He needs not only to be served but to serve, to love and to be loved. Besides the co-operation of others he wants their companionship. He is, though in varying measure, a gregarious creature, sometimes more happy in a crowd than when long alone, and obtaining satisfaction from feeling at one with a group. Few do not require sympathy or seek for understanding. The approval of others or of another is one of man's most urgent demands, which may perhaps be called a basic need. He sees himself reflected in their eyes, and one of the

[1] D. W. Harding, *The Impulse to Dominate* (1941), p. 162.

major facts of his experience is their judgment of himself. He seeks from childhood to earn a favourable judgment. This is clearly in part because he gains advantages thereby, for it will lead those about him to give him what he wants; but in part too it is because he wants their good opinion itself, and wants it for a variety of reasons. Inasmuch as he respects their judgment he finds in their approval that reassurance of his own worth which he is constantly seeking. This gives him a sense of creation and achievement. Insofar too as his affections are engaged he will enjoy the satisfaction of giving pleasure to others, obtaining his pleasure through theirs. It may be also that he gains satisfaction from successful imitation and competition, from proving that he can do what others have done and expect of him. Whatever his motives, whether selfish or altruistic, simple or mixed, there is surely no doubt of his need for approbation.

Equally important is the need to be wanted. The need for affection is closely linked with the need for approval and with the desire to serve. The sense of doing something useful satisfies a creative urge and enhances the personality. The mastery of environment gives a consciousness of power and achievement. The knowledge of being necessary to others has a similar effect, lending him significance, assuring him that he matters. He is ever aware of the group, whether it be family, friends, vocation, church or state, and perhaps few things are more necessary to him than the consciousness of contributing to collective life in one form or another.

Nothing, surely, can be more basic than the maternal instinct. Whether the parental satisfactions are ones of creation or possession or self-denial, it is an important fact that they are vicarious. For this means that one human being can enjoy happiness through the happiness of another, can be and constantly is fulfilled through the sacrifice of a 'selfish' pleasure in favour of an 'unselfish' one. That people need that kind of fulfilment is obvious. From that fact it follows that man needs others to realize himself. While the ultimate satisfaction belongs to himself it is only a peculiarly intense form of something far more general. Indeed affection of any kind has a similar effect on the processes of satisfaction, and it is not confined to the circle of family and friends but may be so extensive as to embrace the whole human race or even all sentient creatures.

Man's need of others for his own self-fulfilment is an element in his nature not depending upon the degree of development of social organization, although this may greatly enhance it, but true of all men as we know them in whatever stage of civilization they may be. It follows that the personal moral ideal, or conception of the good life, must comprehend this sociality. The ideal does not subsist in a vacuum surrounding an isolated individual. It is largely the expression of what emerges from his contact with society. It must include his recognition of the need for others. It carries with it as a corollary the admission of their similar claims. He is entitled neither to shut his eyes to the social facts of life nor to deny to another the claim he makes for himself. It is not a fantasy that he constructs but an attempt to bring order into his experience as a whole, and it must be consistent with itself; it is a rational structure, in short, or it cannot claim to be a guide in a world where causal connections are the only basis of orderly perception. And in this requirement of rationality lies a necessary source of obligation. Inasmuch as his experience proves of men both basic similarities to himself and social inter-dependence the rational concepts in which it issues must take the shape of social ideals; or the way in which he incorporates these facts into his *weltanschauung* may be said to constitute his social ideal.

The requirement that this social ideal must fit the facts of man's social needs and desires affords the answer to the dilemma posed at the beginning of this chapter. We cannot give the same value to the anti-social, as to the social, to a philosophy issuing in perpetual war as to one issuing in social service, because our social needs and desires require us to find the terms on which a satisfactory system of co-operation with others can be secured. Now it is true that the social needs so far mentioned, the individual needs, that is, which involve other people, have not suggested antagonism with others or appeared inherently inimical to social life. The emphasis has been on their possibility of harmonization with one another. Are there not needs, however, of which this is untrue—aggressive impulses, the desire for power and to master others? Do not men sometimes enjoy inflicting pain? Is there not, for instance, what Bentham called the pleasure of ill-will? Are there not competing claims for scarce products? But if these are among the basic needs of which man is aware, and which we must take account of, is not the implication less one of harmony than of inevitable conflict?

It is because of this fact of conflict, because, as Bertrand Russell put it, all human desires are not 'compossible' that we need to agree on principles that will secure the greatest 'compossible' satisfaction of needs and desires. This is in the first place the function of ethics, which Toulmin defines as 'to correlate our feelings and behaviour in such a way as to make the fulfilment of everyone's aims and desires as far as possible compatible'.[1] It is also the function of politics, which may be regarded as dealing with special aspects of that correlation in practice, with that part of the system of co-operation which is concerned with the use of organized force, authority, law, and administration.

The corollary of man's need of others for his own fulfilment is that a way of living harmoniously with them must be found. Some system of social co-operation is indeed implicit, therefore, in the existence of man's social needs, as part of his moral ideal. Just as he has to reconcile his own conflicting needs and desires, and is continually choosing between satisfactions of them, of which often the best that can be said is that one is the lesser of evils; so has he to arrive at some adjustment between his wishes and social claims, not all of which may seem to him to be good, but which he recognizes as forming a part of actual social organization. His response to the actual demands of society may range from active acceptance, to active resistance, in each case based on conscious conviction, but it will probably belong for the most part to some intermediate stage. There may here be passive compliance born rather of habit, conventionality, or imitation than of belief. It is clearly the case that many social customs are continued in this way after the reasons for them have ceased to carry conviction. Sometimes there may be a grudging or doubting acceptance accorded to particular claims on the ground that they form parts, though defective parts, of something which as a whole is regarded as necessary; and conformity in this case, being accompanied by the will to improve, may be thought of as tentative and provisional.

While it is apparent that the accepted system of social

[1] S. Toulmin, *The Place of Reason in Ethics* (1953), p. 137.

co-operation is not a precise or unchanging entity and that there are many possible renderings of it, there are potent forces making for uniformity of interpretation, and so reducing the prospects of social conflict. Between one interpretation and another there is no final objective test because the justification of each, in the last resort, lies in its appeal to the reasoned judgment emerging from individual experience. Implicit in this view, therefore, is the admission of a continuing element of contingent anarchy. The objective good expressed in the actual social order, of the idealist theory, is a chimera which has too often misled people into the acceptance of unnecessary evils and the abdication of the human intelligence from its proper responsibility as the sole force for creating and realising ideals. But the denial of such a single objectivized social harmony need not cause alarm, for the prospect of contingent anarchy developing into actual conflict seems as relatively rare within organized society as it is frequent between organized societies. The explanation is not far to seek.

For within organized society there is a whole system of tradition behind customary behaviour. From earliest childhood the citizen has impressed upon him the accepted stereotypes of idea and expression. He grows up in a world of conventions, learning the importance of conformity and the dangers of being different. At home and at school there is continuously borne in upon him the distinction between what is accepted in his social environment and what is condemned. He is apt to find that agreement is much the easiest course, though he will often discover too that the code he is expected to adopt is different in different places, that the principles among his schoolfellows are not consistent with those at home. But all the engines of education are brought to bear upon him to develop habits of thought and behaviour socially approved in the circles in which he moves. In human nature few influences are stronger than those of habit, and few more difficult to break. As Bagehot saw, the spirit of imitation, especially when combined with deference, is one of the most powerful forces of social cohesion. Both in combination dispense with the need for thought and judgment. Independence in such matters is only too frequently discouraged in proportion to the social view of the importance of the subject with which it is concerned. People are much more readily allowed to have their own views of beauty than of morality, of artistic performance than of social behaviour. The whole force of organized society, with its political machinery, its legal system, its social institutions, its religious bodies, its educational structure, imprints the accepted pattern of the desirable social harmony upon the impressionable mind of the growing child. The miracle is that it ever escapes into any measure of originality or inventiveness. And yet, as it has been the business of liberal political philosophy to argue, humanity has depended upon such rare escape for its movements of progress, for its achievements alike in the moral or political, and the scientific, spheres.

The pattern of social harmony, with all its implications of rights and obligations, which is thus impressed on the citizen's mind when at its most malleable, establishes in it the acceptance of a body of duties incorporated in its social ideal. And 'once the duty is made our own, it becomes as it were a part of our self, so that its fulfilment becomes at least as much the concern of the self as the fulfilment of a wish. This fact that a duty, though originally in a way extraneous to the self, becomes adopted by the self, so that its fulfilment is essential to our mental well-being, is one of the central features of the development of the moral life, and we find references to it, in one or other of its aspects, in practically all the psychological literature concerned with moral conduct, no matter to what school the writer belongs and with what particular problem within the moral field he is immediately concerned.'[1] For such is the process by which the social pattern of rights and duties enters into the personal moral ideal, spreading uniformity of interpretaion and behaviour. Clearly the cause to fear the practical consequences of accepting the validation of social ideals as ultimately a personal one is greatly reduced by this fact.

Besides the influence in the direction of uniformities exercised by tradition, custom, habit, imitation, education and the impact of the accepted social code, there are all the similarities of experience of those who are brought up and live in the same environment. Such are the very foundations of social unity. That is what makes a people. Common geography and language, and shared differences from neighbouring communities em-

[1] J. C. Flugel, *Man, Morals and Society*, p. 18.

phasize the similarity of experience. Conversely, the greater the disparity of experience between different groups or classes within a nation the less is likely to be the agreement of ideas, for underlying that agreement is the fact that similar stimuli tend to react on similarly conditioned organisms in the same way. It is this which makes social behaviour as uniform and as predictable as it is and so, too, makes social science possible. Even though it is true that 'no experience is ever exactly the same to two individuals. The varying content of earlier experiences and the varying physiological conditions assure this;'[1] nevertheless there can be no denying the enormous cohesive influence of common experience upon the members of society. Similarity of experience issuing both in a similar consciousness of needs, and the mutual awareness of similar needs, is one of the most potent forces making for uniformities in the formulation of the social ideal.

It is important, however, to distinguish between such a concept, called a social ideal, which is really a personal ideal in its social application, and the collective formulation of an ideal which is social because it is embodied in institutions having the approval of society. The latter is based upon the former; but it deeply influences the former too. For social institutions, while they are a means for the satisfying of needs, just because they provide a socially recognized channel for satisfying them, direct and canalize them, and may even, as we have seen, to some extent create them. They provide, as it were, an external embodiment of needs which has a suggestive effect upon man, making him conscious of them as needs. In the conditions of modern life, at least, social organization is so necessary a means to providing for their satisfaction that the shape of the provision it makes in large measure moulds their expression, as well as supplying their demands. In this sense it may be said that not only does man need social organization as a means, but that he needs society as an end, that in its very life and structure he is apt to find a necessary part of his own fulfilment, that he can regard it as a projection and enlargement of his own personality.

Being by its nature, as we have said, a co-operative association, the state is ultimately dependent on the removal of con-

[1] E. S. Griffith, *The Impasse of Democracy*, p. 349.

ditions which make co-operation difficult or impossible. This is to say that it is not only to provide an agreed way of settling disputes. Even more important, it must aim at preventing disputes from arising by seeking out the sources of conflict. By building into its foundations conditions directed to the eradication of these it can alone secure the prospect of a stable existence. That is another way of saying that it must embody widely accepted principles of justice. It means that we need to know what are the most usual sources of conflict, and to consider in any particular instance what is likely to be their strength relatively to the forces making for agreement and social cohesion.

It is patent that some of the most probable causes of active disagreement lie in the economic field. Opposition between the interests of land and factory, agriculture and industry, owner and tenant, employer and employed may sow the seeds of a discord emerging as conflict over corn laws, or rent and factory Acts, or which may culminate in lock-out, strike, or general strike. But generally these are not matters in which compromises are unobtainable provided there are stronger common interests, economic, social, national, propelling towards cohesion, and if also there are adequate means of peaceful adaptation and change. It is when they are reinforced by other factors, religious, racial, political, that they may cease to be capable of resolution, or when political rigidities block reform. It can scarcely be doubted, for example, that racial, religious and nationalist factors made a peaceful compromise impossible in the conflict between Protestant English landowners and Catholic tenantry in Ireland, or that there economic conflict exacerbated the nationalist one. Again, economic division may lead to a social division: it may produce, for instance, a cleavage in the educational system and such a contrast between the experience, background, and general way of life of different classes of the population that it renders impossible their effective mixing. Inequality, when it makes the nation not one but two, may mark the absence of any real community at all. When the division between rich and poor is stratified by permanent class barriers of a legal character as in the old régime in France and Russia, or of a social character as in nineteenth century England, it may be thought that the term co-operative association is a misnomer. Quite certainly it becomes so as soon as this hierarchical structure ceases to enjoy an acceptance stretching generally among the dispossessed orders of society. But then, when that is the case, the society is already in a condition of disintegration: the forces of social change are at work to cause the dissolution of one type of co-operative association and its transformation into another, and only the degree of social and political flexibility can determine whether the change will come by an evolutionary process or by revolution. For surely a basic and general agreement as to aims and the methods of achieving them—in other words, that it shall be fundamentally a co-operative association—is a condition of survival, and indeed of the existence of a political society, as of any other association. Locke's doctrine of consent—though it is not the whole story, for the possibility of 'force without authority' qualifies it—expresses an essential truth.

Other sources of conflict, or factors causing division, may create what we call the problems of a plural society. Such are religion, race, language, or a local patriotism associated with a particular region having a distinctive history or tradition. Any of these may set up a group within the larger community whose cohesion rivals, or whose claim to loyalty prevails over, that of the community as a whole. Such differences constituting potential or actual causes of conflict require the discovery of terms capable of reconciling them with the unity of the larger whole. In other words, satisfaction of certain conditions which they create might be the price which has to be paid before the whole can be itself an effective co-operative association. William Pitt recognized that the unity of Canada as a whole required the constitutional acceptance and defence of basic racial and religious divergencies within it, and not until these had been embodied in a federal structure covering their protection was the overriding unity of Canada as a political entity able to prevail. Similarly the price of cohesion in the Swiss Confederation or the West German Republic has included the practice of representation at supreme executive level of regional and either religious or linguistic differences.

VIII

THE CONTENT OF MORALITY: RULES AND VALUES

SOCIAL organization implies rules. These are arrangements through which social life is carried on, and we customarily dignify the more important of them with the name of moral principles. It is germane to any enquiry into political foundations to consider what these are and how they are to be explained. For political studies are concerned with special parts or aspects of social organization, which, being only parts, require to be seen in relation to the whole if they are to avoid distortion. We have sought to avoid that particular distortion which results from confusing the state with society—of which it is but one aspect. By defining the state as one particular kind of association for the co-operative pursuit of common ends, among many kinds, we have rejected that view of it according to which its ends exclude all others, so that it is beyond the reach of social rules and moral principles. Since, on the contrary, it comes within the realm of these, the student of political theory cannot escape the necessity to consider what they are.

The matters with which political studies are concerned, such as the constitution of the state itself, government and administration, the making and enforcing of law, the organization of common services, are indeed parts of a whole system of social co-operation. Any such system, being an attempt at devising a way of living and working harmoniously together, must express a large agreement about the ends and methods, or terms, of social co-operation. How these ends and methods are related to the satisfaction of needs, and how usefully they can be formulated in concepts such as self-realization, happiness, or the good life, is what we have been considering under such headings as the criteria of purpose, reason, and the bases of morality. What a society must seek to create, in order to survive, is a common corpus of values. It is the consciousness of shared acceptance of these, and of mutual respect among its members for their contribution to the realization of them, that makes a viable political community.

What is the nature and extent of this large agreement about the terms of social co-operation, this agreed content of morality, this accepted view of the social good? These are really three aspects of a single question. Having seen something of the conditions and limitations which beset the way to objective definition, we may now consider how far it is possible to give an acceptable answer. Treating the question, then, as a triple one, we shall first relate it to moral principles regarded as rules of behaviour. Secondly we can consider how far these may be linked as a corpus of values, and this may take on a form which might not unsuitably be called a social *weltanschauung*, all the more since it often attempts to place them in the wider setting of religious or philosophical belief. Then there is, thirdly, the concept of a definitive social good; this is clearly related to the first two, in some measure summing them up and formulating them into a moral imperative, or at least a signpost to guide action.

(a) Rules of Behaviour

Moral principles can be properly regarded as rules of behaviour; as such they are clearly terms of the system of co-operation which we have taken to be aimed at making for a compatibility of fulfilment. They are not, however, simple, self-evident absolutes from which specific deductions are to be made, but a product of experience in which we must seek both their rationale and the basis for the precise details of their practical application. It is these by which they gain the precision necessary to fit them to the practical needs of social life. To see them in this way is to take a surer step to secure their observance than to attempt to instil them as unexplained absolutes.

The keeping of promises may be a moral rule, or term of

such a system, but we need to know why it is a valid rule, and only in the process of examining the reasons for it can we come to understand its force and the limitations which must be set upon it, in common with other rules, when we come to applying it in practice; to see why it should be generally obeyed and why on some occasion it should not be. Without such understanding it may share the aridity of the uncomprehended taboo operating on the basis of fear; with understanding it may serve to integrate behaviour with convictions in a fertile way. Besides, only in this manner can we appreciate the development that occurs in moral principles. For the content of morality is not static. It is neither absolute nor perfect. We can only treat it dynamically and assess improvements in it if we see it as a rational structure, and as directed to agreed ends.

It is no derogation from promise-keeping as a moral principle to say that the reasons for it are ones of social convenience. On the contrary, by fitting it into a rational structure founded on agreed ends the effect is to strengthen it. Indeed if we could never rely on people to keep their promises social life as we know it would be rendered impossible. Nothing could be planned in advance. No agreement to meet, to let or rent, to work or employ, to buy or sell, would be worth making. We accept it as a duty to keep our word because we recognize the advantage for social relations of reliability and predictability. Because we want to be able to depend on the undertakings of others, we therefore recognize the value of the principle. That is to say we admit the obligation to observe it, and the propriety of laws and customs defining and enforcing it. Evidence of its value as a principle is the fact that we seek to avoid as much as we can dealing with people whose word we cannot rely on. Our obligation to obey it is supported by the implicit threat of social ostracism if we do not. Because of its importance to social life we regard it as right that the state should concern itself with promise-making to ensure, as far as its sanctions can do so, that promises are kept. The whole law of contract and much marriage law has this character.

Much the same can be said of the duty to tell the truth. It is a more satisfactory social arrangement than its obverse, because it makes for reliability and predictability and avoids the waste of time in doubting and checking. We soon cease to wish to have dealings with the person whose statements are intended to mislead us, for we find it too tiresome continually to have to sort out the false from the true. Although the art of blarney has its devotees it is a sterile and time-wasting one. Etiquette, it is true, often dictates falsehood, and consideration for others may cause them to be misled for what is thought to be their own good, but it is arguable that in most cases the truth would be more salutary and social life in the long run more comfortable and predictable were the conventions on the subject to be grounded less on the easy lie, and more on moral courage. There are plenty of good reasons for the habit of speaking truthfully. The person who tells stories which would be entertaining if they were true becomes a bore when they are not. The habitual liar ceases to be believed when in fact he tells the truth. Highly apposite is the sad fate of Belloc's Matilda, who 'every time she shouted "Fire!" They only answered "Little Liar!"' and who perished because no one believed her. For much of the dependability of social relations is the result of mutual reliance on truth-telling, and liars succeed only when they can take advantage of the habit of such reliance. That was the basis of Hitler's argument for 'the big lie', that if it was big enough few would disbelieve it, but insight into its effects in the ultimate undermining of all confidence in leadership was denied him, as was appreciation of the extent to which actual refusal to disbelieve was dependent upon the previous observance of the principle of truth-telling.

The law has less to say about truth-telling. To assist the administration of justice it punishes severely for perjury, and it also imposes penalties for misrepresentation for profit and for malicious defamation, but, on the other hand, it is not strange to the idea 'the greater the truth the greater the libel'. So it would seem that we have here another case of approaching a moral principle from the angle of its consequences, judging it by the criterion of social convenience. But perhaps there is room for more clarity of thought on this subject and more agreement on the rationale of the limits to set upon it as a term of social co-operation. Certainly this is so with regard to its relations to politics. What part does it play in establishing the personal reputation of a leader? How important an element is it in successful propaganda? To what extent can the appearance of telling the truth be reconciled with the reality of not doing so? When the answers to Pilate's question are buried in the separate languages of expert elites what safeguards are available to the lay public?

But perhaps the nature and rationale of a moral principle can be more readily seen and more dramatically illustrated in relation to the fundamental and universal rule, 'thou shalt not kill'. Obviously in some form or other this is a principle necessary to social organization, a basic term of all social co-operation, an imperative of behaviour in society. The reasons for the other principles of promise-keeping or truth-telling we sought in the field of social convenience. It did not seem necessary there to go beyond the terms necessary to social co-operation and appeal to the intuitive perception of an objective moral absolute. While this also made it possible to contemplate limitations upon the application of the principle, to regard it as an absolute would not. But this character of moral principles is shared by 'thou shalt not kill'. The justification for it must also lie, that is to say, in reasoned argument appealing to preferences, it is not an absolute moral truth beyond discussion; yet just this authority is what is often claimed for it, in common with other moral truths.

But we have only to remember how readily this simple and universal principle can dissolve into an exhortation by the most authoritative mouthpieces of the social conscience to do the opposite in order to realize how much it stands in need of rational analysis. For, once such a principle needs to be qualified and to be said to apply only in certain circumstances, or to certain classes of people, it must cease to be a clear moral imperative. With each new qualification there is more room for doubt, because argument has to be undertaken and judgment exercised. The claim will be made, for instance, that it does not apply where life is threatened, when states are at war, under a tyrannical government, under the rule of some particular kind of wickedness, or to bring about or to prevent some special form of revolution. Questions of interpretation then multiply. To kill when the life of the agent is threatened or the life of another and if so what others? To kill on behalf of 'my country right or wrong', or under what form of tyranny, or to prevent a usurpation before it has taken place? Any attempted rephrasing—

such as 'thou shalt not kill save when no other course is possible without endangering another life or the safety of the state or without allowing the creation of a worse evil'—has none of that immediacy of acceptance implicit in the claim to a self-evident certitude. The necessity for such a rephrasing, however, does bring out the considerations which are really involved; it does refer us to the terms of social co-operation, to the ends for which men co-operate in societies, to the conditions which experience suggests to them as required for their living and working harmoniously together. Besides, it surely gives a more realistic account of what happens in a world where the several states of the United States, like the British episcopal bench and political parties, are divided on the merits of the death penalty.

For what we are really seeking to do is to fit this, and other principles like it, into a larger rational structure, where we can see it as an element in a coherent system of values. Because we attach superlative importance to human life and happiness, we seek as guides to conduct those which will best promote them, or least detract from them. Forcible interference of any kind with human freedom is an evil, and therefore to be kept to a minimum. Whether it amounts, at one extreme, to a minor and temporary restraint or, at the other, to the taking of life, it is only to be justified by its ability to secure a greater good. The same principle is applied to the constable making an arrest and to a lawful government faced by rebels or an invading enemy: to use 'the necessary force'. And the same line of argument is appropriate to the measurement of penalties for crime—that they should be the least necessary to achieve their primary object of deterrence. The question how best to implement any such principles may certainly produce disagreement, but since it can be put in factual terms it can at least be discussed with some hope of practical solution.

Examples may also be taken from the field of sexual morality. Here in particular, owing no doubt to both their importance for happiness and the strength of the passions they arouse, have rules been dogmatically enunciated. Treated as principles beyond the necessity for argument they have been established as categorical imperatives to be imposed with the help of social sanctions, and the result has only too often been to divorce theoretic assertion from practical acceptance. Only when they are seen as rationally conceived guides to happiness, or as conditions of happiness empirically determined, is this divorce ended. Then, for instance, the nearly universal rule against incest ceases to appear as an unexplained decree, and is seen as arising out of the requirement for preserving the stability of family life. Similarly rules against adultery, which show much greater variety, instead of being rested on authoritative dogma can claim rational acceptance as being grounded in the need and desire for permanent marital relationship and the demonstrably damaging effects of its breach upon this. And 'thou shalt not commit adultery' is transformed from a commandment, rested on fear and aimed at restraining 'natural' desire, into a commonsense guide to behaviour, grounded in demonstrable psychological facts in the field of the causation of attitude and habit, and which by rationally establishing the behavioural conditions of happiness tends to direct desires along channels leading to its achievement. Psychology is so young a science that it is hardly surprising if we still use methods of guidance for determining the terms of social co-operation which belong to the dark ages preceding it or if we have so largely failed so far to adapt our principles and values to the enlightenment it offers for our use.

The analysis of what we are doing when we assert moral principles or values may also be clarified by way of contrast. We may compare our own with the different assertions of the past or of other societies, and so bring into relief the important points in our own agreement. Thus we regard the principle of 'a tooth for a tooth' as a primitive conception of justice, and have refined the idea of requital for injury from one of inflicting an equivalent degree of damage on the guilty party into one of making him give the sufferer an equivalent compensation. This seems to us a refinement because we consider the idea of reciprocal damage inferior to that of compensation as a method of promoting happiness. We no longer accept the view that the heathen should be exterminated or the 'true faith' be enforced by the sword because we deem it manifest that truth cannot be secured in this way. Slavery we reject because we have extended the definition of desirable freedoms, strengthened the belief in equality, and diminished the relative emphasis on property rights. The long-standing institution of war is no longer accepted by many communities as a satisfactory, or 'thinkable', method of settling their disputes. There are signs that in the relations of many of them it has already been relegated, like trial by combat, to the limbo of the irrational.

And when we turn to comparison with other societies we can again find contrasting illustrations. Buddhism regards it as a moral principle not to take intoxicants. Much opinion in the west—not least T. H. Green's—would agree. If total abstention is not a part of western values this cannot be because we lack evidence of the evils of excessive addiction to alcohol. We just do not happen to have had a taboo of religious or superstitious origin associated with this particular question, and so, in contrast to those questions where we have, it has been more possible to consider the matter 'on its merits', that is to say by rational examination of consequences in terms of human happiness. But whatever the outcome of such consideration, a prohibition or an approval or an injunction to moderation, it indicates what we have insisted is the essential character of such 'guides to behaviour', that they are not self-evident assumptions but products of reasoning; and whether we came to the same conclusion as the Buddhist in this matter or not, he and we would both be aiming at the same result.

(b) *An Agreed Corpus of Values*

Thus though it is a mistake to conceive of morality as an absolute beyond argument; not subject to the test of consequences or requiring the support of reasoning from experience, nevertheless, there is widespread agreement on the content of morality. It is worth considering both the character of this agreed content, and the processes leading to it, and we have been doing so in regard to rules of behaviour. But such rules fit into a larger complex which tends to give them coherence and greater strength. This complex has the character of a system of values. As we have said, it may be called a *weltanschauung* because it expresses a general body of beliefs, and indeed we find it given such labels as 'humanism', 'the Christian ethic', 'the Buddhist philosophy', or 'Marxism'.

But about the values within such a complex as that held by

a 'civilized society' like America or Britain, one preliminary fact is patent—that there is often agreement on a general idea as expressed by a vague word rather than upon the precisions through which alone it can be practically realized. When it is remembered that freedom, for example, has been defined as anything from obedience to law at one extreme to absence of legal restraint at the other, and indeed recent logical analysis has shown the confusions to which careless use of it may lead,[1] it must be clear that there is not a conclusive guidance for particular situations to be derived from agreement upon its being a good thing. We should be wary of too readily thinking that there is. But that is by no means to deny all significance to the community of approach it expresses. Men have been trying to define 'justice' at least since the great debate of Plato's 'Republic'; but since there would be much agreement today on what things should be called just and what unjust—although it must be admitted that there would also be some disagreement —there is real point in the view that it represents an accepted value, however imprecise or difficult exactly to define.

For it is both true and important that, as Leonard Woolf argues, 'there has developed an ethical corpus of values which stands in a similar relation to individual and social life as the corpus of contemporary knowledge. Each is reciprocally both cause and effect of the stage of civilization which at any particular moment a particular community has reached. Neither has the validity of absolute certainty or absolute truth, and it is highly probable that if we attempt to prove to a complete sceptic that freedom is good and should be treated as a social end by governments . . . we shall reach a stage in the dispute in which each is relying on a belief which he cannot prove logically or scientifically. Yet the sceptic, like Hitler and Stalin, when he is off his guard or not influenced by some ulterior motive, will implicitly admit the validity of these "civilized" values.'[2]

It is true, again, that there is a wide content of moral agreement which can be expressed in general terms such as these, as used by Leonard Woolf. 'When we think of "civilization",

---

[1] See, for instance, M. Cranston, *Freedom, a New Analysis* (1953).
[2] For this and the following quotations, see his *Principia Politica* (1953), pp. 91, 255, 268.

we regard happiness, freedom, humanity, and justice as essential ingredients of the "civilized" way of life. . . . A civilized society is one which provides a way of life which conforms to certain standards of social value almost universally recognized. . . . And the judgment that these ingredients are good is so firmly planted in the minds of 20th century men that, as with happiness, so with freedom, say, or justice, rulers or governments which in fact are destroying freedom or doing injustice on a vast scale, are forced by the profundity and universality of those ethical beliefs to pretend or even to believe that the slavery or injustice which they are inflicting is "real" freedom or "real" justice.' Or, again, 'Philosophers, from Plato and Aristotle to Hume, Mill, and Professor G. E. Moore, have disagreed profoundly with regard to the meaning, origin, nature and validity of our ethical beliefs or judgments. Yet despite this wide disagreement, they hardly ever disagree about what is good or has value. . . . The philosophers, like the kings and dictators, show that it is not doubt or disagreement about what is socially good or bad which causes rulers or governments to do what is evil according to the canons of social value established by civilization.'

This last point, however, is surely exaggerated. We are not casting any doubt on the superiority of 'civilized values' when we admit, as we must as a fact, that contrary values are or have been genuinely accepted. It may certainly be doubted whether Hitler or Stalin ever really did accept the values to which Woolf alludes. Did they not, at least, attach a superior and overriding validity to other values, such as the interests of the state or the race or the revolution? We are, of course, perfectly free to condemn this even while admitting its genuineness.

For we may well ask what it is that causes men, whether rulers or not, to do what is evil according to the 'canons of social value established by civilization'. May it not be that they wish to enforce what for us today are unaccepted values, of which history offers plenty of examples? Such was the putting to death for heresy by the Catholic Inquisition or the Calvinist Consistory, the Bolshevik killing of Kulaks or capitalists, the Nazi butchery of Jews or socialists, or even perhaps—though certainly a less barbarous crime—the deporting of the pioneer trade unionists by an English government representing primarily its landed gentry. But is not each of these justified to those who do the evil as in accordance with values they accept, the defence of religion or of property, or of the communist or Nazi state?

We say that they are wrong. Indeed no 'civilized' person today would doubt that they are wrong. And in doing so he would not be stating a mere dogmatic preference for other values; rather would he be reasoning from experience to certain conclusions upon which these other values were based: that men cannot be forced into religious belief, that the evidence for the belief is inadequate, that conformity imposed by fear is unconvinced and unenduring, that respect for human life and freedom of association is the condition of a society in which it is comfortable to live, that the justification for the employment of power over men can only lie in the acceptability on such grounds as these of the ends to which it is directed. In arguing like this, however, he will only be doing what we have been endeavouring to do here, that is in the analysis of human needs and purposes to seek the basis and character of their moral ideas. What makes the result a corpus of values is that it is thus built up as a reasonably coherent interpretation of experience; however much it may express agreement it is thus no dogmatic assertion of an orthodoxy.

That there is such agreement is of great importance, but it is also important to see that it is the fruit of the many judgments of 'civilized' men concurring in their preferences, valuations, reasonings about means, and conclusions as to desirable terms of social co-operation, rather than an assertion of absolutes expressed in a determinate, comprehensive and recognizable code; in short, that it springs from contemporary experience, knowledge, belief and reasoning, and consequently is largely dependent on how far these in their turn are shared. It has much in common, it is true, with thinking over the last two or three thousand years, but the degree to which it is common, especially in particular applications, can be easily exaggerated. There may be wide agreement, for instance, in supporting 'justice', 'freedom', and 'equality', but what these meant for an ancient Greek, an early Christian, an Italian of the Renaissance, or mean for a twentieth century Englishman, American or Russian may contain deep-seated differences. Nor sometimes is what they mean for people of different classes the same. Another value, property, may even empty them still more of agreed content. So contrasted may be the experience of the member of a family wholly dependent on wages, and of one with a comfortable patrimony, that it issues in no common interpretations of such concepts, but rather in ones that each deny those of the other. The economic structure of a society will determine the class divisions within it, and they in their turn its complex of values. Indeed, 'the qualities that help to confer social status give a broad indication of the society's prevailing values'.[1]

In any modern community, moreover, there are varying patterns of value held by groups or sub-groups within it contending for dominance. There is, for instance, the importance of the value-pattern of the businessman, with its original association with the Protestant ethic, as a moulding influence on the corpus of values of American society. Here the belief in self-help, hard work, free enterprise, independence of social aids, whether received or given, in not being dictated to, in success gauged in terms of money, wealth, and a home and wife suited to its more impressive display, has its counterpart in the disparagement of other less competitive and less material values accepted by other groups and societies. Similarly British society has had its corpus of values much influenced by a group pattern in which the chief emphasis was laid on the team-spirit, conformity, and unconcern with ideas, art or scholarship. Both these examples illustrate what is probably more general, indeed, 'a deeply entrenched feature of western societies: the tremendously high value placed on the individual's contribution to the material prosperity of the group, in spite of the lip-service paid to other values, such as art, scholarship, religion, social wisdom, moral development.'[1] Such facts as these are sufficient to suggest that there are inadequacies, and a certain amount of fluidity, in what is accepted as the current corpus of values of a 'civilized' society.

It is important not to underestimate the significance of such limitations upon the definitiveness of this; for there are frequently ways in which the complex of values of even quite an

[1] D. W. Harding, *Social Psychology and Individual Values* (1953), p. 166.
[2] *Ibid.*, p. 74.

I

advanced society fails to meet the needs of many of its members.[1] 'The question for a social group is whether it enforces an unnecessary and disabling degree of isolation on some of its potentially valuable members.'[2] This is apt to apply especially to such people as writers, artists, philosophers, scientists, whose activities lay more stress on individuality than on the central stream of social life. People who find that the values of society are uncongenial to them, being frustrated by them, are both a standing testimony to its incompleteness and a continuing weakness and threat to its survival, for it is to them that revolutionary movement makes its primary appeal. 'At any given period in the history of a culture some people will be concerned with unfashionable, disparaged or uncomprehended values and will be subject to social deprivations not because they are 'socially maladjusted' in some morbid way but because their contemporary group is relatively insensitive to the range of values that means most to them. We are brought back to the fact that social groups are likely to fail a proportion of the members they produce and to make the psychological conditions of social life wastefully hard for many people whose work is eventually recognized as a valuable social possession.'[3]

Similarly those who are frustrated because the corpus of values does not provide them with the sense of having a function in the life of their society, either because their activities are not socially acknowledged as significant or because social organization fails to offer them the opportunity of useful activity—as is the case with the unemployed or a submerged class—will also constitute a standing criticism of society or even, maybe, a dissident element threatening the stability of the whole. It is no accident that the existence of frustrated groups—like factory workers or intelligentsia in Russia—has preceded the totalitarianism which overthrew much of what we should accept as belonging to the corpus of civilized values.

The importance of recognizing these limitations is due, secondly, to the danger involved in too ready an ascription of 'objectivity' to what a 'civilized society' accepts. For this is an

---

[1] E.g. of William Morris and Burne-Jones conducting 'a crusade and holy warfare against The Age'. J. W. Mackail, *The Life of William Morris*, Vol. I, p. 63.
[2] Harding, *op. cit.*, p. 76.
[3] *Ibid.*, p. 79.

invitation to another form of social and political authoritarianism, when a dominant group claims final knowledge, as it is apt to do, of the 'canons of social value established by civilization'. Better though they may seem, they are imperfect and in continuous need of improvement, which is often only to be obtained by dissidence, sometimes by defiance. Indeed, their fundamental contrast with totalitarianism lies in the fact that they must be built on this right to dissidence. Their authority is derived not from 'brain-washing' designed to confirm official revelation, but from the clash of freely exercised judgment often expressed by groups diverging from the main stream. Totalitarianism's denial of this as the basis of authority is the primary objection to it; not to what it teaches, but to the claim that this is an absolute, which consequently ought to be imposed.

But a 'civilized society' very easily falls into just the same error of claiming that its 'established' values ought to be imposed, though the error takes a different form. It may be less apparent that they are being imposed at all if the sanctions employed are social rather than political. Tolerance, it must be remembered, is no natural characteristic of man; nor is it an easy growth of society, but the product of a developed culture, only to be maintained at the cost of constant vigilance. Intolerance of deviation is not the exclusive prerogative of governments using the powers of legal enforcement and the state mechanisms of propaganda and indoctrination. The tyranny of custom and public opinion may also be a grave danger.[1] Indeed, it may be a worse threat to liberty, even though its sanctions are not those of the state but of society, because of its tendency to dictate a more personal range of values. Contemporary civilized thought is certainly critical of most of what might be called the Hollywood stereotype of values, despite their wide acceptance; as well as of much that a dominant bourgeoisie would assert to be 'established', and the imposition of which takes place through a whole complex of social pressures. The criticism is by no means confined to what politically authoritarian regimes enforce by the use of state power.

Nor would it be realistic to think that what is thus enforced

[1] As Mill recognized in his *Essay on Liberty*. He remarks for instance, 'Wherever the sentiment of the majority is still genuine and intense, it is found to have abated little of its claim to be obeyed'.

in the one-party state is not accepted before being enforced. If the opponent of totalitarianisms imagines that their teaching is not widely believed, but is invariably spoken with the tongue in the cheek, he is living in a realm of fantasy. For they just do not accept his scale of values with anything like the order of priority he gives them, however clearly he may think that this is demonstrated or 'established'. He makes a dangerous mistake in so imagining because this may lead him to attribute to totalitarian faith a brittleness that is not there. On the contrary, it is apt to be held, perhaps because of its claim to concrete objectivity and absoluteness, with a faith and conviction often absent from the competing rationalist doctrine with its greater uncertainty about what can be regarded as 'established civilized' values. That is why it is imperative for the character and strength of this doctrine, with its firm rational foundations, to be as clearly understood as possible.

We think it absurd that totalitarianism should lay down *ex cathedra* what is good music, art, or literature, because we recognize such aesthetic judgments as the province of private taste and not of authoritative decision.[1] Our objection is not that we disagree with the actual verdict, but that it is claimed to have been made finally and objectively for us. Our objection is just as strong, indeed, in those cases where we come to the same conclusion. What we claim is the right to record our own reaction to the experience of a musical, artistic, or literary work. That is not to say that the canons of aesthetic merit, any more than the canons of moral value, cannot be discussed in such a way as to evoke a large measure of agreement, but it is to assert that both in the last resort are subject to private judgment and can acquire validity only from agreement among persons making the judgment, not from any public act 'establishing' them. But, as Westermarck remarked, society is apt while admitting the subjective and relative aspects of aesthetic canons to ascribe objective and absolute qualities to moral criteria.

---

[1] Though the operation of the censorship taints us with the same brush. Among scores of possible instances, consider the fact that for half a century (apparently because it contained scriptural characters) 'Salome' could not be publicly performed in England. Although it is said to be the main ground of Wilde's international reputation, and was given a famous rendering by Sarah Bernhardt, its author's fellow-citizens were not permitted to judge its merits for themselves. See also Chapter I of my *Reactionary England*.

Such doctrines of absolute or intrinsic values risk having a demoralizing effect because of their tendency to divorce the good from the test of everyday experience, and so to erect it into an ideal to be preached rather than one really capable of being observed. We are familiar with the Victorian who, analysing on Sundays the meaning of a moral rule by reference to divinity, could behave on weekdays in another world where empirical criteria apply. We see him as a split personality, with a mind divided into uncommunicating compartments, whose verbal professions and actual deeds belie each other. Such a lack of integration between professed philosophy and daily behaviour is the very antithesis of morality. And this antithesis may be produced no less by relying unquestioningly on the authority of the 'accepted' than of some 'inspired' text, substituted for the teaching of experience operating upon a mind open to its constant reassessment. A doctrine requiring acceptance on authority tends to remove one of the twin essentials of morality, an open and enquiring mind, and to weaken the conviction attaching to the other, that is the observance of the ideals resulting from unfettered reflection. In other words it positively discourages the growth of morality by thwarting, and causing to atrophy, the machinery of intelligent valuation. Morality laid down by authority provides its own nemesis.

Moreover, the spirit of tolerance which is a condition of the spontaneous development of moral values, is necessarily inhibited or destroyed by authoritarianism. An attitude of tolerance is also a condition for the successful working of systems of social co-operation, and so authoritarianism is clearly guilty of a tendency to remove their foundations. If we want to promote the spread of morality we must encourage what morality is based on, the free development and application of values, even though they are dissident values. 'The authoritarian believes in discipline as a means: the libertarian in discipline as an end, as a state of mind.'[1]

It is true, of course, that the valuations of the ordinary citizen would be wholly inadequate without the tutoring of the many groups to which he belongs. We all have much to learn about the ordering of individual and social life, for which a lifetime is not enough, and should be lost without what is taught in

[1] Herbert Read, *Anarchy and Order* (1954), p. 27.

childhood or later drawn from the accumulated wisdom of mankind. Much of this is expressed in the different brands of ethics, philosophy, and religion. Only when any of these demands—as, when 'established', it is apt to do—that we accept its teaching on faith or by authority does it constitute an evil defeating the essence of the service it otherwise can render. Provided that the appeal of such doctrines is to free judgment, and their lessons are submitted to the test of experience they can greatly promote morality. They may meet our need for teaching, but that need at the same time invites abuse.

(c) *A Social* Weltanschauung *or Established Religion*

This need for teaching is not merely for moral precepts nor even for a corpus of values, but it often takes the form of a demand for a comprehensive philosophy capable of giving them a more convincing and enduring quality, a *weltanschauung* which puts the whole of experience into some sort of order. Behind it lies, that is, the wish to find an explanation of the universe. Historically men have sought that explanation in magic, religion, philosophy or science, or a combination of them, and always they have linked the government of the universe with their view of morals and politics. It is no accident that absolute monarchy coincided with the picture of the world as ruled by a Jehovah who governed mysteriously and capriciously, or constitutional monarchy and the rule of law with a view of the world as a mechanical system, or totalitarianism with a nihilistic belief in might as right and brute force as the basic element of creation.

There also lies behind it men's yearning to escape from the mutability of all they cherish. In transience they long for permanence, for certitude in the realm of the uncertain, and amid a hostile nature for security and peace. So it is not difficult to understand why man takes refuge in religion, which gives him the solace of these things.

Many societies have some sort of religious system performing such services as these. There is a double reason for this fact. Not only does it meet these needs and longings and provide, as it were, a map of the universe; but, when allied with secular authority, it strengthens the institutions of civil society and the

THE CONTENT OF MORALITY: RULES AND VALUES 135

fabric of law. To the human sanction there is added the divine. The jurisdiction of the courts applies the law of nature which in turn expresses the decrees of providence. Behind the law is morality and behind morality revelation. The church lays down the law in one field, the state in another, and alliance between them helps to maintain a settled order of ideas and institutions. Each reinforces the other. Each helps to avoid the challenge to its authority which would follow the development of a different system of ideas. For there cannot long subsist together a conflicting philosophy and politics. Inasmuch as politics is a branch of ethics, the requisite unity between them must be somehow secured.

So it is not surprising to find a firm *weltanschauung* collectively held and authoritatively interpreted as the characteristic of an ordered society. Nor would it be untrue to say that it has generally been founded at least on an averagely good scientific approach to knowledge for its time and place, and an averagely wise valuation of conduct and estimate of consequences. So that for most people of its day to adopt it is likely to be reasonably satisfactory, that is to say, to give a sufficiently acceptable explanation of the universe, and to provide a code of behaviour coming near enough to a good way of life, as they see it. It comes to be believed therefore that the authority of this and obedience to it is the condition of any kind of moral order or stable society. And indeed it may well help, though the penalty of discouraging the free application of reason to experience is both stultifying to scientific or moral advance and discouraging to morality itself. In some degree the cost of social stability thus achieved is, that is to say, moral decay. At least insofar as the dissident element is not allowed to work out its own salvation is the possibility of progress and the degree of total fulfilment in the community reduced, the amount of frustration increased.

Now this social *weltanschauung* is institutionally expressed, in the history of many societies, in such things as an accepted religion, an established church, a theocracy or even a modern totalitarianism. The social moral code is built upon it, to which is married a state-imposed system of law. There is thus developed an interlocking pattern of ideas and institutions wherein fundamental beliefs support authority and dictate obedience to the social moral code. The modern state enters into the inheritance, imposing it through law, society expressing it in custom which it stamps with the seal of public opinion. The corollary of this development is that the conviction should grow that each is necessary to the other. It is thought that without religious belief there would be no social order and that the penalty for the loss of established certainties is the decay of morality, where in the long run the opposite is the truth. An accepted religious system with the promise of rewards or the threat of punishment in the next life, is considered the condition of decent social behaviour and obedience to law in this life. These sanctions of proper conduct are regarded as an essential foundation for social order imbued with purpose. And the acceptance of any moral values is thought to be conditional upon acceptance of a single established faith. Upon that depends the ability of society to curb man's natural wickedness, his destructiveness, his selfishness, and all his anti-social tendencies.

But this settled order of things of the closed society has now long been in decline, with the ideas on which it was based. Societies in transition, like Britain in the last hundred years, are apt to be marked not by one but by several competing kinds of *weltanschauung*. This was clearly true of the England of the nineteenth century, where they corresponded to deep class divisions. Still dominant, though increasingly challenged, was the upper class belief in a natural hierarchy, in status tempered by duty and privilege by charity, in the Church of England, and in a certain implicit intimacy between Queen Victoria and the Almighty. Middle class nonconformity held the more dynamic faith that providence helped him who helped himself, revealing its mysteries through the inner light of the individual conscience; and it set a higher value upon the qualities and behaviour that lead to material success. Of the urban working class, on the other hand, certainly no reader of Henry Mayhew could imagine that a large part of it accepted either attitude, or, indeed, any significant portion of what were currently regarded as Christian values.[1] Seen in retrospect, the settled order of nineteenth century society seems neither very settled nor very orderly. Theology was failing to hold its own against the on-

[1] See K. S. Inglis, *Churches and Working Classes in Nineteenth Century England*, Historical Studies, Australia and New Zealand, Vol. 8, No. 29, for an interesting expansion of this.

THE CONTENT OF MORALITY: RULES AND VALUES 137

slaught of history and science. Upon truth by authority there was more and more successfully supervening the claim of freedom of thought. Until today the edifice of civilized values, like that of knowledge itself, is increasingly seen as the work of the individual intelligence which works in co-operation to produce a whole that is never static, never complete, and always subject to the constantly renewed test of experience, the continual moulding by reinterpretation. This is perceived to be a process of friction and conflict. In it there is no stability and no certainty. And the result by those who hanker for the past settled and established system is not unnaturally attacked as a 'collapse of values'—because it represents a wholly contrasted approach to the world about us and to our relation to it.

The full significance of the contrast, it is true, was not immediately, or even speedily, seen by the critics of the notional settled order of the closed society. They believed rather that the religious and supernatural certitude which they attacked could be replaced with a similar certitude by the science which they upheld. For they did not realize the whole implication of the fact that the postulate of science was an empirical method demanding an open mind and precluding such certainty. In fact, as so often happens in the history of thought, they continued to be influenced by the assumptions of the system of ideas which they had discarded. Victorian agnosticism, for instance, sought in the law of evolution a metaphysical sanction for ethics, and this gave it 'the appearance of a new nonconformist sect'.[1] The earlier rationalist too was making an unconscious metaphysical assumption of the simplicity of the truths relating to man and to the universe in order to attack theological and metaphysical mysteries. 'Assuming human nature to be a simple thing, the Enlightenment also, as a rule, assumed political and social problems to be simple, and therefore easy of solution. Rid man's mind of a few ancient errors, purge his beliefs of the artificial complications of metaphysical 'systems' and theological dogmas, restore to his social relations something like the simplicity of the state of nature, and his natural excellence would, it was assumed, be realized, and mankind would live happily ever after.'[2] For this reason upon which this

[1] Cf. Noel Annan, *Leslie Stephen* (1951), p. 221.
[2] Arthur O. Lovejoy, *The Great Chain of Being* (1942), p. 9.

contrasted approach to the world about us is founded has a double meaning, as Dewey observed in the quotation already given but worth repeating. 'It designates both an inherent immutable order of nature, superempirical in character, and the organ of mind by which this universal order is grasped.'[1] The ambiguity has had misleading results. The former meaning contains a metaphysical assumption of which political science needs to beware. It refers us to the reason or the 'intellectus' of the scholastics which is bound to come to a predetermined result, and not to the intelligence which performs its activities of empirical reasoning whether or not the consequences of doing so are to expose a postulated 'universal order'. We are not likely today, however, to imagine that this latter process achieves to absolute certitudes, or is uninfluenced by the economic, social, and psychological conditions in which it operates.

For what emerges is that, while there is much agreement, there is also disagreement, on the nature of, and the social means to, happiness and the good life. There are preferences and scales of value variously held at different times by different groups and societies. Each wants to follow its own and regards its own as the guide to good and happiness. Such are the data with which politics must work. When confronted by these differences its answer lies not in the idea of a superempirical or intrinsic good which ethics shall provide, or in demanding from philosophy the result of a search for final causes. For politics the answer is rather that 'Since men are largely alike, in spite of all other differences, in seeking for themselves the freedom to live as they each prefer, the principle of freedom of choice is the only principle which can plausibly be made a universal basis of decision. . . . In the last resort political decisions are to be justified, not by the various ends or ideals which they may be supposed to serve, but by the relative freedom of choice which they allow to those whose lives are most affected by the decision.'[2]

Freedom thus becomes both a term of the system of cooperation for the pursuit of common ends, and a claim upon which only the demonstrable requirements of that system of co-operation can justify limitations. Equality rests similarly on

[1] J. Dewey, *The Quest for Certainty*, p. 203, and above.
[2] Stuart Hampshire in *The Listener*, May 14, 1953, p. 799.

the absence of any generally acceptable case for inequality. The demand and desire for the good life as they see it, and for a political and social organization in which it is secured, experience shows to belong to all men as men. It is not equal treatment in that case that needs justification but unequal treatment. Not of course that the principle of equality, springing from men's equal demand for self-satisfaction and fulfilment, implies standardization. Difference of interest, size or capacity, for instance, must logically interpret equal treatment in different cases as meaning 'technical' rather than 'higher' education, or unequal sized shirts, or pianos rather than television sets. For lack of uniformity of treatment is here justified by reference to the same principle, equal claims to the opportunity for the good life as varyingly envisaged. If, on the whole, the views of modern civilized men are that neither custom, creed, class, colour, race, wealth nor birth provides any self-evident case for privilege, although it is true that there are groups, or whole communities even, who have denied, and some still deny, each of these views, then it is because each denial in turn lacks the basis of certainty by which alone we could justify inequality. In short, the terms of our system of co-operation must include the assertion that we cannot refuse to one the opportunity to realize his purpose which we allow to another save on grounds which are common to all. And when we add that such refusal to others could mean the same refusal to us, we are merely putting the statement another way, though it may carry more immediate conviction because we know that this opportunity is what we ourselves want more directly than we know that it is what another wants.

Our conclusion then about the content of morality is that it does not consist in pre-established or superempirical certitudes. The life and movement of society rest on freedom of thought and experiment inconsistent with any such determinism. Its stability is not a matter of discipline imposed by authority and resting on rules discovered by revelation, but of agreement that particular forms and methods of co-operation are the most satisfactory because they best promote personal responsibility and best allow for the pursuit by each of the good life as he sees it. There is the need for continual adjustment of the interpretation and the means for this. It is true that there may be conflict, and that the agreed system of co-operation requires the backing of sufficient power to ensure its preservation and adaptability. If there is instability inherent in this, what Laski called contingent anarchy, it must be not only recognized as inevitable but welcomed as the sign of a living society. It should be welcomed as best guaranteeing the release of men's creative energies. Only by recognizing both their responsibility for constructing values and their necessity to obey them can society promote morality. In doing that it makes happiness the definitive social end. By contrast, the stability that is based on alleged certitudes, as we find it in closed societies, is seen as at the same time unreal, and insofar as it is temporarily imposed with success, so imposed only at great cost in suppression of responsibility and understanding and in consequent loss of satisfaction. Nor is there any reason to suppose that the sanctions of conduct are strengthened by the authoritarian assertion of dogmas to which men only pay lip-service because they do not stand up to the test of experience or because men are not allowed the test of alternatives. Men demand and need each to create his own constructive ideal and reflect it in his individual and social way of life. It is the business of the system of social co-operation to promote this.

IX

THE SOCIAL GOOD

THE idea of an overriding obligation to 'the social good' is very generally to be found in political theory. Thus T. H. Green says that 'every virtue is social in the sense that unless the good to which the will is directed is one in which the well-being of society in some form or other is involved, the will is not virtuous at all.'[1] And H. J. Laski speaks of social good as 'such an ordering of our personality that we are driven to search for things it is worth while to obtain that, thereby, we may enrich the great fellowship we serve.'[2] There is a difficulty, however, in the imprecisions of these phrases. For we need to know what we mean by 'the well-being of society' or what 'it is worth while to obtain'; nor is it clear whether 'the great fellowship we serve' is confined within the state to which we happen to belong, comprises the whole of humanity, or is some intermediate combination of communities.

For much caution needs to be exercised in the use of this idea. Some indication of the way in which the concept of the social good can be acceptably envisaged should have become apparent from our consideration of the nature of moral principles and values and of the way we arrive at them. This showed them as the outcome of reasoning based on preferences. It would make the social good rather like a pyramid founded on individual valuations. There are contrasting views, however, which, as it were, stand the pyramid on its head, and start from the needs of society, or social habit, or the inherited social environment, in order to produce from this something which it is believed has an objectivity impossible to achieve otherwise.

[1] *Works*, Vol. II, p. 550.
[2] *Grammar of Politics*, p. 25.

But the danger of these is that they tend—albeit often unconsciously—to a new form of idealist theory, substituting the herd for the state as the expression of the absolute, and attributing to its needs or behests an *a priori* pre-eminence. Social good then becomes whatever custom demands. Or it may be whatever the interests of the nation dictate. J. A. Hobson once made what is essentially the same contrast, criticising the social psychologist, William McDougall: 'Instead of regarding a nation as an interaction of minds for certain definite co-operative purposes, Dr McDougall tells us that "the nation alone is a self-contained and complete organism: other groups within it do but minister to the life of the whole—and when the nation is regarded from an enlightened point of view, the sentiment for it naturally comes to include in one great system all minor group-sentiments and to be strengthened by their incorporation. . . . Loyalty to the nation," he adds, "is capable of exalting character and conduct to a higher degree than any other form of the group spirit".'[1] In this illustration we are confronted by just that arrogation of an *a priori* pre-eminence to a particular exposition of the social good, namely in this case the national interest, against which it is important to be on guard.

This also typifies the widespread assumption that there is special virtue in this kind of conformity to something judged to be an objectively determined pattern of the social good. But the validity of this assumption is open to question. Does not the orthodox extolling of individual adaptation to society lead to a thwarting of the development of personality and the creative urge, the principal source of every victory won by man over his environment; every enlargement of human freedom?

'In our opinion there is no warrant at all,' write K. Walker and P. Fletcher,[2] 'for the assumption, which seems to be implicit in a great deal of contemporary religious teaching as well as in many current psychological theories, that while the Self-Urge is the manifestation of our lower animal nature, the Social Impulse is altruistic and morally superior; with the corollary that the achievement of complete sociability is the fulfilment of personality or that good citizenship and spiritual integrity come to pretty much the same thing.

[1] *Free Thought in the Social Sciences* (1926), p. 255.
[2] *Op. cit.*, pp. 62, 63.

'On the contrary . . . the more exclusively and simple-mindedly men and women apply themselves to the task of adapting themselves to their social environment the more likely they will be to lose whatever personal reality and spiritual integrity they ever had. At any rate, that is how things seem actually to be going, for as Joseph Pieper, the Westphalian philosopher, has lately pointed out: "more and more, at the present time, 'common good' and 'common need' are identified, and (what somes to the same thing) the world of work is becoming our entire world; it threatens to engulf us completely, and the demands of the world of work become greater and greater until at last they make a total claim on the whole of human nature."[1]

'Moreover we do not think there can be any doubt that if today this process of adaptation does in fact mean that the individual is lost, submerged in the amorphous nonentity of the herd until nothing but the gregarious urge is operative in him, it is because, in obedience to the Self-Urge, he plays for safety first, last, and always.'

Attempted 'objective explanations' of the social good also tend to submerge the individual in the herd. Man regarded as possessed of will and purpose distinguishing him from his environment becomes part of an undifferentiated mass, an element in a mechanical process. It is the penalty of the machine-metaphors used for social description that they carry implications of human impotence, and so encourage attitudes of resignation to what is falsely conceived as inevitable. Similarly, behavioural studies facilitated by the statistical development of the social sciences, with their suggestion of predictability, seem to imply a social determinism in which individual will and purpose plays no part—unless it is realized that what they are doing is to describe this very operation of will and purpose as it proceeds within a group. When reason is thus used as an instrument of 'objective explanation' and not as a dynamic instrument for adapting means to ends, it suggests the impotence of the will. The tendency in the development of modern scientific thought in the social field which studies man as part of the universe, dethroning him from his place of honour in which once he spoke of 'the world and I', has been to discourage the

[1] Joseph Pieper, *Leisure, the Basis of Culture* (Faber, 1952).

view of him as a creature with the unique characteristic of purpose of his own, with the freedom to choose well or badly, and the power largely to determine his own fate, and to make him appear a part of nature subject to contingent laws. The existence of an immanent social order or a transcendental moral order can alone imply such impotence of the will. It is essentially against the sterility and sense of impotence produced by such an approach to society that such a revolt takes place as is represented by the Sorelian plea for the morality of action and violence. Only when it is remembered that social morality is nothing if not the compound of individual moralities, deriving its authority therefrom, and not conferring authority thereon, can this fatalistic acquiescence or its converse, the worship of action for its own sake regardless of aim, be escaped.

A parallel search for theoretic objectivity is to be seen in the attempt to produce the foundations of political theory out of pure description of social habits. Thus Dewey seems sometimes to deny much of the significance of mind, and particularly anything that can be called individual mental activity, as determining social ends and defining the means of their achievement, and produces instead implications of social automatism.[1] He claims 'to show why the psychology of habit is an objective and social psychology', and to use this approach as the proper basis for political theory. In *Human Nature and Conduct* he writes:[2]

'The traditional psychology of the original separate soul, mind or consciousness is in truth a reflex of conditions which cut human nature off from its natural objective relations. It implies first the severance of man from nature and then of each man from his fellows. The isolation of man from nature is duly manifested in the split between mind and body—since body is clearly a connected part of nature. . . . It is fair to say that the psychology of a separate and independent consciousness began as an intellectual formulation of those facts of morality which treated the most important kind of action as a private concern. . . .

'Any moral theory which is seriously influenced by current

---

[1] It is true, however, that he treats this question somewhat differently in *The Quest for Certainty*, Ch. X.
[2] Pp. 85, 86, 87.

psychological theory is bound to emphasize states of consciousness, an inner private life, at the expense of acts which have public meaning and which incorporate and exact social relationships. A psychology based upon habits (and instincts which become elements in habits as soon as they are acted upon) will on the contrary fix its attention upon the objective conditions in which habits are formed and operate.' And he goes on to speak of 'the profound importance of unconscious forces in determining not only overt conduct but desire, judgment, belief, idealization'; and also of the 'practical realization of the dependence of mind upon habit and of habit on social conditions.'

No one today would deny the importance of the influence of habit, social conditions, and unconscious forces on mental activity; but they are influences and not the total of mental activity itself. They always leave something out. For we know that different men and societies respond to similar situations in different ways. Even if we could know all about the habits and conditions of a society to which a man belongs, and the unconscious forces they may generate in him, we should still not know with any assurance how he will think he should act or how in fact he will behave. Qualities peculiar to him or to society may be more significant than characteristics he or it shares with others. The knowledge of an individual or a society must cover not only 'acts which have public meaning' but the 'inner private life' or lives from which they issue, which they affect and are affected by; for through these alone can they attain any meaning at all. 'Public meaning' cannot exist apart from, but only as an addition of, estimates of meaning arrived at by separate consciousnesses.

If political theory were really to accept the obvious and basic fact of the existence of the separate consciousness of each human being as the 'intellectual formulation' of an irrelevancy it would be denying a part of reality and so be in danger of being divorced from reality as a whole. If it treats the individual as irrelevant to it, he is likely to regard it as irrelevant to him. While it is true that each man's 'body is clearly a connected part of nature', so is each mind, which is an aspect of each body; and conversely, while there is a separateness about each mind, so is there about each body which, after all, moves, lives, feels grows, and dies on its own. And to regard this essential character of it as an 'intellectual formulation' is to exchange the real for a notional abstraction which makes it so much the less relevant to the world of actual experience.

The description of social habit is important to political science because it may produce serviceable generalizations on probabilities in social behaviour. But it cannot illuminate the meaning or value of behaviour; for this we cannot be content with describing habit or similarities of behaviour, but must deal with the purpose and effects of behaviour. And this means evaluating the good aimed at and the results of behaviour in terms of the good thus sought. Whether the good under discussion relates to 'acts which have public meaning' or to an 'inner private life' this remains true. Morality—and, therefore, political theory—is concerned with both. It deals, indeed, with their purposive integration. It may not discard one half of the equation, being concerned with the acts of men not merely as events, but to discern in them the content of meaning which makes them significant.

At the root of attempts at 'objective explanation' of social good is the belief that it is possible to avoid the uncertainties thought to follow from the admission of a subjective element into the analysis. But the quest for certainty in these matters is, as we have seen, something of a wild goose chase. Yet it is just this that objectivity seems sometimes to be thought to mean— an absolute imposing itself on acceptance. Such a definition contrasts with a proper understanding of objectivity as we find it, for example, in Bertrand Russell. 'A doctrine,' he writes, 'is objective if it follows, by arguments generally recognized as valid, from facts not thought open to question.'[1] For this definition, on the contrary, lays a necessary emphasis on general recognition, or not thinking open to question, in other words on processes into which judgment enters.

Judgments are the results of interactions, of experience on the one hand, and interpretation on the other. When we look at the things on which judgment is exercised we see an objective source, when at the things performing the judgment a subjective source. And the use of the term 'subjective' may be no more than an attempt to emphasize the latter aspect; but it does not follow

[1] B. Russell, *Human Society in Ethics and Politics* (1954), p. 121.

from the fact that an external object is common that the interpretation of its effects, or even the experience of it is invariably also common. This may have importance, it has been suggested, even in the exact sciences. It is especially important where we are concerned with the judging of values into which enters an element of desire and preference. And in our concern with the relations between individual and society it is doubly vital. Here the stress on the individual and the subjective is rendered the more necessary by the tendency of the social sciences in their effort to discover generalizations valid and useful in societies to lay too much emphasis on the other side of the interacting processes.

A similar point is made by D. W. Harding. 'Social adjustment,' he writes, 'should be understood as a mutual interaction between group and individual. One of the pervasive pseudo-problems of psychology arises from the difficulty, in our structure of language and thought, of talking about a reciprocal process of this kind without phrasing it in terms of one side or the other. We are tempted, for instance, to say that the organism responds to environmental stimuli; only to meet the contrary assertion that environmental events would have no stimulus value but for the needs of the organism to which they relate: and though we may take refuge from this difficulty by emphasizing that the organism and environment together constitute a field of forces we are not thereby provided with words and grammar that allow us to describe particular features of the interaction without starting from one side or the other. The individual's relation to his social environment provides one form of the general difficulty, and until we have mastered a new grammar for discussing interaction we must verbally misrepresent the process by making subject and object out of the equal interacting forces. To counteract the usual emphasis on the individual's adjustment to his group it may then be worth while phrasing the mutual relation in terms of the individual's requirements of his group.'

We see the same difficulty in Dewey's analysis of 'the construction of good'.[2] Criticising the sensationalistic theory which makes the origin and test of ideas subjective, he says that 'it

[1] *Social Psychology and Individual Values*, p. 56.
[2] Chapter X of his *The Quest for Certainty* (1930).

failed utterly to account for objective connection, order and regularity in objects observed. Similarly, any doctrine that identifies the mere fact of being liked with the value of the object liked so fails to give direction to conduct when direction is needed that it automatically calls forth the assertion that there are values eternally in Being that are the standards of all judgments and the obligatory ends of all action.' He continues: 'Without the introduction of operational thinking, we oscillate between a theory that, on order to save their concrete and human significance, reduces them to mere statements about our own feelings.'[1]

But it is clear that Dewey does not thus dismiss subjectivism. The distinction he draws between the statement that a thing 'satisfies' and that it is 'satisfactory' is important: the first may be the report of an isolated fact; the second involves consideration of the thing in many aspects, in relation to other alternative things, to consequences, to the question whether it will continue to satisfy: it is an interpretation of experience and judgment of value by regard to purpose, indeed an application of a *weltanschauung*. However, it thereby becomes objective only to the extent that there is agreed recognition that facts and arguments are valid; and since the facts in this case are apt to be value-judgments it continues to be tied to the subject who does the considering and judging according to his own views of more permanent satisfaction.

But Dewey's contribution is instructive. Let us look at it more closely, even though to do so properly it must be quoted at some length. He says that he does not object to an empirical theory, of which utilitarianism is a type,[2] 'as far as it connects the theory of values with concrete experiences of desire and satisfaction. The idea that there is such a connection is the only way known to me by which the pallid remoteness of the rationalistic theory, and the only too glaring presence of the institutional theory of transcendental values can be escaped. The objection is that the theory in question holds down value to objects *antecedently* enjoyed, apart from reference to the method by which they come into existence; it takes enjoyments which are causal because unregulated by intelligent operations to be values in

[1] *The Quest for Certainty*, p. 251.
[2] *Ibid.*, pp. 245-9.

and of themselves. Operational thinking needs to be applied to the judgment of values just as it has now finally been applied in conceptions of physical objects. . . . Escape from the defects of transcendental absolutism is not to be had by setting up as values enjoyments that happen anyhow, but in defining value by enjoyments which are the consequences of intelligent action. Without the intervention of thought, enjoyments are not values but problematic goods, becoming values when they reissue in a changed form from intelligent behaviour. . . . Formal analogy suggests that we regard our direct and original experience of things liked and enjoyed as only *possibilities* of values to be achieved; that enjoyment becomes a value when we discover the relations upon which its presence depends. Such a causal and operational definition gives only a conception of value, not a value itself. But the utilization of the conception in action results in an object having secure and significant value.

'The formal statement may be given concrete content by pointing to the difference between the enjoyed and the enjoyable, the desired and the desirable, the satisfying and the satisfactory. . . . To say that something satisfies is to report something as an isolated finality. To assert that it is satis*factory* is to define it in its connections and interactions. The fact that it pleases or is immediately congenial poses a problem to judgment. How shall the satisfaction be rated? Is it a value or is it not? Is it something to be prized and cherished, *to be* enjoyed? Not stern moralists alone but everyday experience informs us that finding satisfaction in a thing may be a warning, a summons to be on the lookout for consequences. To declare something satis*factory* is to assert that it meets specifiable conditions. It is, in effect, a judgment that the thing "will do". It involves a prediction; it contemplates a future in which the thing will continue to serve; it *will* do. It asserts a consequence the thing will actively institute; it will *do*. That it is satisfying is the content of a proposition of fact; that it is satisfactory is a judgment, an estimate, an appraisal. It denotes an attitude *to be* taken, that of striving to perpetuate and to make secure.'

Now, although all this is true, it might be said that it protests too much. There is not quite all that difference between satisfying and satisfactory. If the two concepts can thus be contrasted, they are also linked. A thing cannot be satisfactory unless by and large it satisfies. The satisfaction cannot, to be adequately understood, be treated as something isolated in time or unrelated to the person enjoying it. It depends not only on the past to be a satisfaction in the present but on the future too, on experience of the former and expectation, derived from it, of the latter. The present enjoyment of it is only a fleeting moment through which the future becomes the past. To say it satisfies is no more than to seize upon a single point in a series of events. And so it is also true to assert that a thing cannot satisfy unless by and large it is judged by the subject to be satisfactory. Moreover, if the two concepts are thus linked to one another, they are also linked to the subject which receives, records and evaluates the satisfaction, just as they are to the objects which occasion it. Thus the concepts satisfactory, desirable, etc., are not independent of individual experience and judgment in each case. The objectivity of their content depends on the common recognition of values and is limited so soon as they are thought open to question. As John Stuart Mill said, 'the sole evidence it is possible to produce that anything is desirable, is that people do actually desire it.'

The order and regularity which it is feared subjectivism lacks is to be found, and only to be found, in any observed similarities within the interactions of subject and object. It relies, that is to say, on the extent to which similar objects and events produce similar, though distinct, experiences and judgments.

Of this we must revert to two points of which the fundamental importance has already been claimed. The first is the significance of the part played by what we have called the reason and Dewey the intelligence in this process of valuation underlying morality, which thus ties it as much to the individual as to the object. It is a necessary part. Without it, as he rightly insists, satisfaction is not a good. What he calls 'operational thinking' is precisely this process by which the reason of each is applied to the past experience of each so as to bring order into his present and future activity. That, we have argued, is the foundation of the course through which morality, satisfaction, happiness, self-realization, or the good life is achieved.

The second is the equally important fact of the very considerable agreement which issues from this process of operational thinking as undertaken by civilized men. This is the common content of morality as it is conceived in contemporary society. But it should be said at once that it leaves no room for the contrasting notion of goods which are 'intrinsic', that is, which have no necessary connection with any act of intelligent valuation. For a value to be intrinsic it must be based on one of two concepts both of which are unacceptable. Either it expresses the ordinance or nature of a metaphysical Being; or it expresses the ultimate reality of a natural order imposing itself on men. G. E. Moore gave a good examples of this latter formulation when he laid stress on two such 'intrinsic' goods: personal affection and the appreciation of beauty. Of the former, the religious formulation, an example is Canon Raven speaking of such 'intrinsic' goods of Christian philosophy as love, faith, charity, humility—to which he opposed with contumely the idea of satisfactions as equivalent to the narrowly egoistic aim of 'having a good time'. What has been asserted here is the contrary view while denying that it has any such narrow implications. It has been said that we find things good because they satisfy, that we value them because they meet some need we feel, that they express our choice or preference, that we prefer them because they fit our designs; not that it is they which create our purposes; that the only common content of morality is the expression of agreed preferences. And when we agree, as most civilized men largely do, with Raven and Moore in preferring love, beauty, humility, it is because, and only inasmuch as, these seem to produce the most fully and permanently satisfying way of arranging our life.

This is not, of course, to belittle the religious or other apostles of the doctrine of human frailty. It is fully admitted that we pursue pleasures which do not satisfy. We give way to momentary impulse and cause hurt, which we regret, to ourselves or others. We concentrate interest on the diminishing returns of self and find ourselves cheated of the wider interests that others enjoy. We cut ourselves off from the service of others and discover that we are alone. We fail to develop our perception of beauty and lose aesthetic delights. We overestimate our merits and importance and are disappointed, unsuccessful, humiliated. We are self-satisfied and do not gain the advantages of improvement. We shut our eyes to the unfamiliar and forfeit deeper insight. We seek transient pleasures at the cost of satisfactions that endure. We often fail, that is, to act intelligently or rationally. But the consequences of failure underline—they do not deny—the importance of the rational test.

In our attempts in the twentieth century to give meaning to the social good or the well-being of society we need to make the eighteenth rather than the nineteenth century our starting point, while remembering nevertheless the lessons and warnings to temper its optimism with which the latter should provide us. The age of enlightenment set its faith in the powers of human reason. It saw man as infinitely capable of controlling his environment. He believed in himself. By the sole use of his own powers of thought and organization he could dominate circumstance. To him alone belonged reason, wisdom, and power. But the result of this liberation of the human mind, and the experience of what it could do, was to subject it in the nineteenth century to a new kind of tutelage. Man produced industrial society only to fall down and worship the machine he had made. So astonishing was the magnificence of his own handiwork, indeed, that its demands seemed to Herbert Spencer to constitute an imperative beyond question, by which alone the rights of man in society could be defined. Men discovered the law of evolution and so established the impersonal rule of the survival of the fittest in a preordained competitive struggle. They developed an economic science wherein 'economic man' was caught in a mesh of supply and demand determining, without the possibility of his effective intervention, the productive and distributive processes of society. This economic configuration of society determined in turn its political design. Man's fate lay not within their own power but was the outcome of inevitable processes and blind forces. The advance of historical study revealed patterns in history and men as subject to laws of historical necessity, as bound, in obedience to a pre-ordained and mechanical law of inevitable progress, to 'let the great world spin for ever down the ringing grooves of change'. With the growth of psychology and sociology man's spiritual autonomy is invaded by revelations of the importance of herd instinct and mass suggestion, and what he had imagined to be his own ideas and beliefs appear as the product of primitive urges, subconscious drives, or social and economic conditions. The individual becomes a statistical unit in a physical mass. Useless for him to say, like the frog, 'I am myself alone,' for what matters is not he but the genus or the species. We start not from him but from the mass, the group, the herd, the class of which he is interesting only as a type. Romantic concern with personality gives place to concern with 'forces', none the less inhuman for being 'social'. Man feels himself to be not the master, but the creature, of circumstance. The result of his emancipation is that he exchanges one servitude for another, that of his own social inheritance.

And this is not less the case when that inheritance is not a traditional order but a revolutionary one. It is no more useless to maintain that traditions are made and changed by human volition than to protest that the Bolshevik revolution, the so-called Marxist revolution, is a complete denial of the doctrine of economic determinism. If ever there were a case where the system of production did not determine a society's political superstructure it was that of the Russia which emerged from the October revolution: rather was the reverse the truth. What relevance has the Soviet Union to the economic relationships and property arrangements of the Russia which gave it birth, save that these set the stage and supplied the possibilities for Lenin to use? No one could be more a utopian than Lenin—in the sense of Plekhanov's definition of the utopian as one who seeks to create a perfect social organization on the basis of an abstract principle. Never, surely, was there a clearer case of the will and purpose of a few reshaping a whole political and economic system, by their skill in using opportunities to realize plans that existed only in their own minds.

The social good in any given society is a mental construct of its members. It is a term of art for something which is a product of human contriving. We should no more expect it to have only one form—which would supply us with that clear source of overriding obligation sought by political theorists—than we should expect Velasquez and Van Dyck, or Picasso and Annigoni to produce the same portrait. There are many different interpretations of the social good given by different societies. Varying concepts of it, and of the best way to achieve it, exist in the minds of the various people, groups, and parties who comprise any particular community.[1]

Yet these differences do not deprive us of all criteria for judging its acceptability as a scientific concept. There are certain things which a portrait must do if it is to be admitted to be a portrait at all. And many of those factors which we have said do not automatically produce a single identifiable object, 'the social good'—such as social needs, habits, instincts, traditions, environment, values—nevertheless have their bearing on, and may set limitations to, what can be admitted as the social good. The criteria for what can be so admitted, however, are to be sought under the guidance, not of a nineteenth century determinism looking for laws of historical inevitability in some unifying principle, such as biological evolution, inevitable progress, dialectical contradiction, economic necessity, but rather under the guidance of the rational and romantic of the eighteenth century who stresses personal responsibility and social co-operation. For those who live in the complex modern industrial society and social service state surely it is clear that the means for delineating social good, or the wellbeing of society, must be sought in the purposes embodied in the system of co-operation, and the methods and forms this takes. These purposes can have meaning only as belonging to, and directed to giving satisfaction to, the persons whose coming together produces the system of co-operation with which the social scientist is concerned. Nor is it enough to say that the social scientist, 'by regarding human life as consisting in the activities of a number of organically related instincts, or dispositions, is bound to interpret the desirable life, or human welfare, alike for individual and group, in terms of the due satisfaction of these instincts'.[2] The defects of such an approach, like those of the quantitative utilitarianism which it resembles, lie in its tendency to omit persons. What is important is the study of the institutions in which co-operation expresses itself, seen in relation to the ends of the persons in whom instincts or dispositions can alone be organically related. 'What has to be

[1] The 'public interest' may similarly be identified with consumer interest, balance of interests, the democratic method and so on; and these conflicting definitions make it useless as a tool of political analysis. Cf. further on this F. J. Sorauf, 'The Public Interest Reconsidered,' in *The Journal of Politics*, Vol. 19, No. 4.
[2] Hobson, *Free Thought in the Social Sciences*, p. 170.

satisfied is not particular impulses or urges or desires, but persons, and persons who are members of societies, and what they require is a way of life in which their different impulses find expression and satisfactions in ways which are compatible with one another and with similar satisfactions by other people. This is what the systems of institutions of different peoples are trying to provide.' And it is by that test alone that we can determine the extent to which the social good is being realized. For this implies a harmonizing of purposes. Because it makes the realization of personality the overriding end, it admits as justifying limitations on this only demonstrable incompatibilities, and so must refuse the presumptive claim of any determinist pattern whatever its basis.

[1] A. Macbeath, *Experiments in Living* (1952), p. 138.

X

THE STATE
AND SOCIAL PURPOSE

POLITICS becomes, then, the study of co-operation in a particular kind of social structure, called a state. But if it is mainly concerned with the institutions and procedures of the state, this does not mean that its interest lies only in the demands of the state on the citizen, of the government on the subject; nor, on the other hand, does it lie only in the claims of the individual or the group against society and the organs which register social decision. What it does mean is that politics deals with both, with duties as much as rights, and rights as much as duties. It must consider the demands of individuals and groups, and authoritative decision as this expresses them or influences them. It examines the pressures exercised in both directions, the interactions of such forces; and because of its need to explain these pressures it must seek to understand the ideas and values which give them their motive power.

Because political studies are intended also to produce recommendations upon how best to deal with such pressures they must be expected not only to explain them but to appraise or value them, and thus to suggest guiding principles for political action. Since, as Sidgwick says, politics endeavours to 'determine what *ought* to be, as far as the constitution and action of government are concerned, as distinct from what is or has been',[1] it must investigate the criteria of moral judgment and deal with ideas of purpose. We have discussed above[2] how these questions may be approached, and it should now be possible so to frame our conclusions as to make them usable as tests for practical application.

[1] H. Sidgwick, *The Elements of Politics* (2nd Edn.), p. 7.
[2] Especially in Chapters II and III.

Society in its political aspect, the state, is at the same time an instrument for the co-operative achievement of satisfactions, a structure through and within which to build the good life, a response in its traditions and institutions to a need for the social embodiment of their ideals which men widely feel—although, of course, it does not follow that any given state necessarily achieves that embodiment. It is important properly to define the state. Equating compulsion with government is naturally linked with a wrong definition of the state. To treat it as unique in that it is solely concerned with power is to invite error by confusing means with ends. Its purpose is to do things or prevent things, for which on occasion the use of force may be necessary. As soon as it is seen not as unique but as just one association of men for achieving their purposes, and so with organization and functions subordinate to these purposes, it becomes rather an agency of co-operation—to which it is true certain elements of compulsion may necessarily attach—and not a leviathan divided into a sovereign power and subjects owing it absolute obedience, joined together by unilateral compulsions.

This latter definition of the state was suitable enough to serve most of the requirements of political discussion when territory and people were regarded as the personal appanage of a prince, when the relations between ruler and subject were simply ones of command and obedience, or when the main function of political authority was the maintenance of order and defence. To the complex modern industrial and social service state it is quite inadequate. For this is primarily an agency of social co-operation and its institutions and procedures accordingly must be evaluated by the test of a wider objective.

Sidgwick made that test 'general happiness', saying that 'we assume certain general characteristics of social man . . . and consider what laws and institutions are likely to conduce most to the welfare of an aggregate of such beings living in social relations'.[1] That welfare we have called the good life, treating morality as a concept in which is expressed a major condition of its achievement. Its advantage is that it is a dynamic concept, with men seen as creative agents of a changing synthesis of fulfilment. General happiness suffers when it is interpreted in

[1] *Op. cit.*, p. 11.

such a way as to suggest a commodity which can be doled out according to a scientific plan of weighted parcels, with men as passive recipients, and it is just this interpretation which has often followed from the utilitarian identification of happiness with a sum of pleasures sought as ends in themselves, and resulting from the gratification of rudimentary instincts and needs.

Although there was no logical necessity for this interpretation to be used, it is not altogether surprising that it was, in the social order of the nineteenth century. Just as the eighteenth century ruling class could refer to the lower orders as 'the mob' and be reminded by Byron, speaking in the Lords, that it was the mob who tilled their fields and manned their armies; so the upper middle class, which dominated nineteenth century society, could think of the rest of the people, that is the working class, first and foremost as an instrument of production, spoke of labour revealingly enough as 'hands', and welcomed Ricardo's iron law of wages according to which the level of its remuneration could never rise above the minimum necessary for survival. The masses who made up the bulk of the population could thus be regarded as physical units conveniently alike in composition; and it was already an advance to recognize that their material needs must be met as part of the social responsibility for maintaining order and promoting industrial progress. To elevate that recognition into a social obligation was something of an achievement. Utilitarianism had much to do with it and John Stuart Mill, with his willingness in later life to apply socialist principle to the distribution of wealth, provided the link between this and Fabian socialism.

Not, of course, that the upper ranges of society approached the good life for themselves in the same impersonal way. Material needs had to be satisfied no less in their case, it is true; but the angle of approach is different when, as with them, the good life was considered on the assumption that they were satisfied, and not as being constituted by their satisfaction; for then the preoccupation could be with freedom of choice, with the moral considerations of self-realization, with individual idiosyncrasy or even eccentricity, and personal responsibility and salvation.

Moreover, if it was convenient for the upper class to think of the mass in this fashion, it was also natural that the working class, and those who spoke for them, should emphasize in the main the demand for the satisfaction of material needs, since this was the most urgent necessity at a time when so often they were not satisfied. It was in this way that utilitarianism could lead on to a form of socialism too exclusively concerned with the material condition of the poor, which would logically regard its objectives as achieved if poverty were abolished and the working class brought up to the material standards of the middle class.

But, if such an attitude was ever justified, it is certainly now out of date. With higher and much more widespread mental and cultural development, with much greater productive capacity and knowledge, not only of matter but of man himself and of society, and with the successful attack on the worst forms of poverty, which has occurred in the west and is occurring elsewhere, it is increasingly inappropriate.

A new emphasis is called for; and this can best be sought, not by discarding the utilitarian tradition with the attack on poverty to which it led, and the socialism into which it developed, still less by decrying it, but rather by looking at it afresh in the light of twentieth century needs and knowledge. This directs attention to elements in it which have tended to be overlooked or under-emphasized. For one thing, it originally recognized the importance of personal valuation in the estimating of pleasures or satisfactions. For another, it was as much an attack on privilege, on the claims of authority to determine what should be sought, on power without social function, on reward incommensurate with service. And there corresponded to these negatives, on the constructive side, the demand for emancipation, freedoms, self-government, equality of opportunity, and much else for which the welfare state has now come to stand. While the combination of forces let loose by utilitarian radicalism on the one hand and, on the other, by the economic determinism of Ricardo and Marx, with its stress on the conflict of classes, and its use of the historical approach that utilitarianism lacked, produced that element in socialism which made fighting poverty its chief aim, there were always other elements which may now seem to us of no less importance. Above all there was that profound respect for human personality which was one of its principal sources of inspiration. This found one of its first formulations in Mill, but was to maintain its force, finding renewed expression in widely different writings from Green to Laski. There was the idea of brotherhood and social responsibility in the Christian socialism of Kingsley and Maurice. There was the desire for beauty, grace, and colour expressed in the work and teaching of William Morris. There was the conception of co-operative commonwealth in Robert Owen. Alike these shared the aim, in the words of Morris, 'to make life happy and dignified for all people.' And in all of them was the same emphasis on the autonomy of personality.

That is why it may be better to use terms, when discussing the test of social objective, which direct attention to the whole personality as a self-directed, and self-integrated complex of needs, and the subjective source of the valuations which give them their potency. That is why, too, it may be better to return to the emphasis on the derivative aspects of the community rather than of the individual, on him as the creator of its activities rather than their object. In fact, of course, he is both; but what this means is that, even when considered as an object, he should not be thought of as a bundle of needs each having a generalized uniformity and each susceptible of treatment in isolation.

This can be illustrated by considering what are the objects and methods of education or psychiatry. Bringing up a child does not consist simply in giving him the correct doses of food, knowledge, and exercise as though he were an impersonal object; it means such things as helping him to teach himself, to face facts, draw rational inferences and think clearly, to evolve purposes and values and a code of behaviour and act accordingly, to understand himself and the world about him, to satisfy his urges and instincts and needs with a due recognition of consequences, to develop his own aptitudes, in short to treat him as a person seeking to harmonize experience with ideas and ideas with a way of life, to find through the development of personal responsibility the way to happiness. When this process has failed and the adult, suffering from 'anxieties', irrational fear, or unresolved internal conflict in a sufficiently extreme form, becomes a mental patient, the psychiatrist again does not regard him as simply an object for drugs, treatments and regulations, but endeavours to find the missing steps in this educative process of facing facts and of adaptation, and retrace them. The therapeutic social club is nothing if not a recognition of the patient as a person needing to develop personal responsibility. It seeks to provide escape from fear and loneliness in the significance of purposive activity, and to cure internal conflict through the conscious integration of experience, ideas, and conduct. This is to recognize in the rational approach the only means of liberation from the fears engendered by the unknown and the ununderstood.

Man cannot live by bread alone, or even by bread and circuses. And our test of social objective, whether it be framed in terms of happiness or of self-realization, must go beyond material need and considerations of 'wealth', beyond physical well-being or 'health', into that field to which past speculation about 'the good life' belongs and on which recent study of mental health throws much light.

Here modern psychoanalysis points the same way. For it stresses the importance of developing an integrated personality: 'a person whose mind has nothing permanently hidden from itself, and who is rational in the sense that the belief-systems governing his behaviour are true within the range of his experience because they have been consistently tested.'[1] This 'healthy mind', consistent with itself and with experience, has clearly much to do with 'self-realization'; it is also clearly a precondition of happiness. Although R. E. Money-Kyrle adds that 'taking the short view, we must admit that we often want to be deluded or, what is the same thing, to be clinically abnormal',[2] it is surely wrong, at least in the long run, to think that 'in a very troubled world, or in a very pathological society, those who take flight from reality may well be happier than those who cannot do so'. He postulates 'one constant motive operating in the direction of integration . . . the desire for truth'.[3] Whether the desire for happiness or for 'truth' in the sense defined above is the stronger, that it should rest on truth is the condition of achieving happiness. Delusion is not a possible

[1] R. E. Money-Kyrle, *Psychoanalysis and Politics*, p. 44.
[2] *Ibid.*, p. 86.
[3] See Ginsberg's criticism of this, *The British Journal of Sociology*, Vol. III, 4, p. 302.

basis. Nor on the psychoanalyst's own showing, is an escapist blindness to the real facts as in such a pathological society as that of the Nazis, or their repression into the subconscious.[1] Such conditions of 'unconscious guilt', 'depressive apathy', 'persecutory anxiety', etc. are certainly not ones of happiness. Furthermore, denial of the unpalatable renders impossible its remedy, the first step towards which must be the recognition of the evil and a rational examination of its causes and cures.

There are practical reasons for regarding as specially important today such an emphasis on individual personal fulfilment as a main consideration for the test of social objective. We see a manifest failure on the part of a very large body of citizens to achieve it. This must surely reflect on the actual organization of society and throw doubt on the adequacy of its institutions and procedures. Moreover this failure is certainly insufficiently realized by those who concern themselves with the analysis of our political and social structure. That there are ten people in mental hospitals in modern England for every one person in prison, or that a single mental illness—schizophrenia, which is one most obviously connected with the problem of integration—fills more hospital beds than cancer, poliomyelitis, and all infectious diseases combined, is surely a fact of special relevance to the social scientist's considerations. Factual and statistical evidence may be insufficient to prove, but there is much to suggest, that neurotic illness is more widespread, just as the suicide rate is higher, in wealthy, modern, industrial societies than in more backward ones less well endowed with material goods, although of course it is not wholly absent from these. It appears that in 1955 in England the loss of time it caused in production was at least twenty times as much as that lost by industrial disputes. Finally, it may well be thought that this is a symptom of a wider failure. For what is revealed to public attention as diagnosed neurotic illness is patently only a part of the total evil: hidden beneath the surface of public recognition may well be the main volume of this particular iceberg. If that were so the failure it represented might even be thought to throw doubts on the foundations of the social order itself, unless of course it could be shown that the origin of mental

[1] Money-Kyrle, *op. cit.*, pp. 74, 84, 100, 102.

illness lay in conditions beyond control. That it does sometimes lie in heredity cannot be gainsaid. But it cannot be questioned either that the causes are often environmental. The truth is that medical knowledge is too incomplete to justify firm conclusions. If we are not entitled, however, to make any such wholesale condemnation of social conditions, we are far from being able to exonerate them; for their relevance is indeed frequently obvious.

The modern political scientist, no less than Aristotle, needs to consider the factors making for personal fulfilment or for what the ancient Greek called the good life. It may not be possible to treat these in any exhaustive manner, but at least illustrations can be drawn showing the relevance of different parts of social and political organization to them. There is for example the relation of the citizen to his neighbourhood or to his work and leisure.

Nothing could show the importance of the first more clearly than the problems attendant on slum clearance and rehousing. Material improvement in the new surroundings has only too often been marked by a net loss of happiness because the old fellowship of the neighbourhood, of informal social groups giving the opportunity of easy intercourse and the sharing of burdens, has given place to aloofness and loneliness. Migration to a better physical environment has been accompanied by the disappearance of a community spirit which, at least as seen in retrospect, more than compensated for the old squalor and overcrowding. There has been a loss of the humour and richness of social contact and mutual help which have been exchanged for impersonal conditions of comparative isolation. Here there is clearly the need to develop the means for removing the barriers to human relationships and for the fellowship of shared responsibility. Social service can help in this. Participation in local authority activities ought to be supremely relevant to it.

It is a paradox, too, of the conditions of life in a modern industrial society that, although they allow greater possibility of leisure and of material wealth than was the case in earlier communities, yet there is more preoccupation today than then with work for production. More thought and energy is directed to this, and less to the intelligent use of that leisure for which there is so much larger an opportunity, less to the knowledge of how best to enjoy what abundance places within reach and to make it contribute to the good life through the enriching of experience and the establishing of enduring values.

Aristotle regarded leisure as the end of toil: we work in order to live; labour is an adjunct to living, producing what is necessary for an existence in which mind and body can be cultivated, sensibility enhanced, enjoyment deepened and extended, and personality developed. But this order of values has been reversed. Acquisitive society respects him who belongs to it less for his knowledge of how to live, less for the qualities of his soul, than for his capacity to produce. Though in the small and equal community virtues of mind and character tell, in the wider society social status and 'success' go to the man who knows how to produce wealth, to organize the production of others, or to manipulate the processes of trade and exchange.

To live for work, rather than the contrary, is at the heart of the Protestant ethic. Leisure is apt to be thought of as little more than a temporary freedom snatched from toil in order to recreate the energies necessary for renewed toil. The years before the capacity to earn a living has been developed are seen as a preparation for earning a living, more than for learning to live; the years which follow retirement as a period of discard and separation from what alone gave life a meaning. The result for those who cannot find sufficient significance in their work is a frustration of their creative capacity, a frustration more characteristic of industrial society, for all its reduced hours of labour, than of the age of individual craftsmanship and closer contact with the elemental realities by cultivation of the soil. Activity loses much of its meaning; life devoted to it has all the less sense of purpose and value. Since men need the satisfaction of doing what is worth while, what has significance, what can be seen to be of service and creative, a society directing itself to personal fulfilment must, in its industrial and complex stage of development, organize work with this need in mind. The corollary is industrial partnership. It is to assimilate as far as possible all forms of economic activity to the professions. That is to say, it is to encourage in each branch of work a consciousness of personal responsibility among all those who are engaged therein, so that they shall be aware of it as a function having

THE STATE AND SOCIAL PURPOSE 165

social import and shall see themselves as sharing in its determination and direction. Of course it must be admitted that not all kinds of work are as readily susceptible of producing a sense of creative contribution as are the professions, and that for many people the most important and satisfying part of life must come from leisure rather than from work. But the lessons of R. H. Tawney's *The Acquisitive Society* have yet to be learnt, and there can be no doubt that their application would do much to help in solving the problem of how to make time spent at work in modern industrial society obtain a meaning and produce a sense of fulfilment which they at present so often lack.

Society must also be concerned with the relationship between leisure and the good life, with the opportunities leisure provides and the capacity to make use of them. It is concerned, that is to say, with education in living as the cultivation and refinement of the faculty to enjoy. Such education aims at the widening of interests, the development of the understanding, and the deepening of appreciation in all the variety of experience. A society geared to production and concentrating its energies on work may be more successful in accumulating wealth than in living. It should remember Midas. The boredom and neuroses of modern civilization look much like the symptoms of the man who knows how to make money, but not how to use it. The restless search for additional possessions or new gadgets produces rapidly diminishing returns; yet it continues to absorb the energies of men and of societies. The capacity for tranquil enjoyment or creative effort whether in the things of the mind, in the arts, or in the things of the body, exercise, games, may be not only not encouraged but positively discouraged by the processes of stereotyping and commercializing. When material accumulation outstrips culture the result is frustration. But always it seems to be to those ideas of fulfilment or happiness, as the Aristotles or the John Mills have contributed to defining them, that we have to return for guidance as to the ends to which social conditions should be designed.

Thus to take personal fulfilment, or self-realization, as our criterion is to encourage the emphasis which actual conditions demand. Needs are the more readily seen as attaching to the personality as a whole, with its interlocking bodily, mental, and social make-up. We can think more easily in terms of action rather than of passivity, speaking of 'urges' which unite the personality and express it as a whole—for instance the creative urge, which combines all these elements, and the satisfaction of which may constitute an important part of fulfilment. Personal responsibility is then more apt to be seen in its proper perspective as the necessary foundation of the standards of value which give cohesion and direction to conduct and a way of life. Its significance can be less facilely lost, on the one hand, in the anonymity of pre-determined causes, often spuriously fathered on a Freudian or Marxist interpretation of causation, or on the other, in the anonymity of the group, whether it be the nation, the trade union or the industrial firm. Nowhere is the contrast we are seeking to make here more apparent than in the revolution in human values wrought by the coming of the industrial age. This industrial age might perhaps better be called the tradesman's age because its values are those of the selling enterprise rather than the craftsman, making a profit being the sign of success rather than creation or service. For it is in this kind of community that the emphasis is withdrawn from personal responsibility. Being in business is no longer equated with performing a personal function in society, with social significance, and does not carry with it the sense of belonging. Personal responsibility disappears into the anonymity of the limited company or the firm. Human values are discouraged or abandoned by the ethic of business. Enterprises become more important, people less important, than before the advent of capitalism.

Fulfilment is thus to be regarded here as being as much a matter of health as of wealth, and health in turn as no less a psychological than a physical product, relying, that is, on 'the healthy mind from which nothing is hidden', and which seeks to generate its own harmony as a way to remove repressions and resolve conflicts. For the healthy mind pleasures are not 'enjoyments that happen anyhow', unregulated by intelligence; their capacity to contribute to satisfaction and therefore their character of being pleasures depends on rational processes by which they are appraised in relation to a larger pattern of happiness, itself reflecting a more comprehensive conception of the good. To employ Dewey's distinction, they must have some claim, not only to satisfy, but to be satisfactory, if they are to be pleasures at all, and certainly if they are to contribute to fulfilment.

In short, the good life seems to consist in a harmony between reflection and action. We evaluate experience, a reflective process of comparing and selecting that brings into play all the capability for imaginative appreciation. From this, partly consciously, partly otherwise, there emerges a pattern of the desirable which may be fittingly called a personal moral ideal. But in order that it shall succeed in producing harmony, this must express a rational attempt at inclusiveness. Every experience omitted, or consequence or causal connection misinterpreted, is a potential source of disharmony. The more it includes, the more it is based on full understanding, the greater is the possibility of harmony. Conversely, the less it includes, because ignorance operates, or wilful blindness, or because of the denial of reality to facts, or of other failure in the reflective process, the greater is the probability of disharmony; and reflection itself, because it is the organizer of consistency, is productive of more or less potentiality of harmony according as it is less or more defective. Moreover, experience must be taken to comprehend not only facts directly recognized, such as basic needs, but ideas taking the form of interpretations of facts by others, and their formulation in abstract concepts, such as principles of justice or articles of religion. The integration of it can therefore be properly regarded as more than a mere pattern of behaviour, although it implies and issues in this, and for that reason it seems suitable to call it a *weltanschauung*, an outlook upon the world, or a philosophy. Nor do we have any difficulty in recognizing the quality of a person who is integrated in this way, whose beliefs and behaviour are thus co-ordinated, and in whom we are conscious that his life is inspired by conviction and ordered by principle. We say that he is at peace with himself. And it is surely correct to claim that in this idea of harmony we are near to the very core of human purpose. True, it is not enough: convictions may be wrong-headed, beliefs irrational, principles narrow, and the result of acting upon them may be anything but peace. It is no less important that they should be intelligent—that is to say, open to reason, admitting the test of experience, seeking to be based on truth—but then that is only, after all, to underline that they must be convictions and not superstitions.

Certain criteria are thus suggested for valuing political institutions and procedures. These must be tested first by the character of the *weltanschauung* they promote in the members of society, and represent as a social product; the comprehensiveness of the experience it embodies and its coherence; and secondly by the extent to which they enable this to be applied in action and life to be lived in accordance with it. In relation to the first test, although we may not expect to be able to pass any final judgment of content, there are useful questions we can ask about its character and there are considerations to afford guidance for appraising this. As it applies to the individual we may consider, for instance, whether it is based on fact or fantasy, or whether it meets needs in a way to produce a satisfactory pattern of fulfilment. We are concerned with such things as the balance it strikes between different sides of the personality, the adjustment it makes between present and future satisfactions, and their range and depth, the extent to which it promotes a harmonious development of the character, and its capacity for supporting a fully satisfying way of life.

In the social manifestation of the *weltanschauung* in any particular community we are concerned in addition with such matters as its understanding of, and method of meeting, human needs, the range of persons to whom it applies—whether for instance it includes citizens of every class and colour or excludes aliens, the extent of its recognition of the possibilities of social co-operation, the values to which its interpretation of experience leads and the ways in which these are embodied in institutions, in short the comprehensiveness and coherence of the system of aims and methods it constructs. From history much can be learnt on this subject, since it furnishes us with many different examples and describes them in operation, thus enabling us often to attempt an assessment of their effects. By the comparative study of institutions, social and political, we may also get not dissimilar types of insight. Thus particular communities can be considered, with their differing methods of understanding and of meeting basic needs, the different moral ideals and political ideologies that issue from them and the varying institutions in which they are applied. It is important, however, that this should not be taken to imply that ideas and institutions can be regarded apart, nor that one has priority of the other. Ideology, that is to say, should not be treated as though it were the creation of behaviour developed by a community subsequently to its customs and institutions to explain and justify them; nor behaviour, customs and institutions as the practical application of *a priori* ideology developed independently; on the contrary, each develops with, and interacts upon, the other; and neither is adequately to be understood in isolation.

The second criterion of political institutions, which we said was the extent to which they enabled the *weltanschaunng* to be applied in action and life to be lived in accordance with it, has clearly a direct democratic implication. Since harmony between the reflective and active sides of the personality must mean conscious direction of activity according to ideas that give it significance, we must have maximum control of our activity. Only insofar as we are able to feel that we share in the decisions that govern our activities, that these decisions are not made without reference to our views, that they are submitted to a process by which we and others like us express ourselves, that they are subjected to a general reasoning upon which we can bring to bear our own, either directly or through our representatives, is it possible for this sense of harmony to develop or this consciousness of personal responsibility. This implies, therefore, what we call responsible government. The citizen cannot be treated as the passive object of decision, authoritative because of its source; he himself is the authority from which its meaning is derived. And every one of his activities requires to be related to the reflective purpose in the development of which he participates. Whatever be the system of co-operation with others of which he is a member—political, social, or economic—what follows is the need for encouraging processes of consultation by which his activities acquire the personal significance which can only be given to them by relating them to his own conscious purposes.

Nor is this process static; rather is it one of continuing adjustment as new experience modifies previous judgment, and modified judgment issues in different experience. It is necessary to ask, therefore, how far such adjustment is facilitated by political institutions, an expanding content of *weltanschauung* assisted and encouraged, or obstacles put in the way of experience and its interpretation. Thus, while happiness, or even pleasure, is not discarded as the clue to what is sought and is judged good, the analysis is pushed further into the nature and conditions of happiness, to make it a more fruitful criterion in political studies. And we seek also to learn about its mutual interaction with changing ideas and institutions.

For political studies are concerned with change both because they are historical or descriptive and because they are normative. In their first aspect it is part of their function to explain social change as an interrelated complex of ideas and institutions. Since, moreover, they seek to offer guidance for the solution of the practical problems in which the act of government is involved, they are concerned with the conditions of development, and the methodology of improvement. How far, for instance, is this a matter of the working out of predetermined causes and how far of conscious direction? The evidence of recent history would seem to suggest that it is increasingly the latter. This being so it is all the more important to underline the necessary concern of the social sciences with the processes of change. Societies today can less safely be treated as static. So the knowledge these sciences provide may have the practical use of showing the means of controlling improvement. Here again we find the importance of the study of co-operation and the expanding avenues of achievement opened up by co-operation. 'Whether or not all life is social in character, it is clear that mental and social development come to be increasingly interconnected. Moreover, beyond a certain point further organization is achieved not so much by changes in the organic structure, as by the building up of structure of a different kind, namely the systems of relationships between individuals which we call social structures. In the case of human societies the most significant change which occurs is the replacement of the mechanism of genetic transmission by that of social heritage or tradition. The new mechanism makes possible co-operation on an ever-increasing scale, and above all it immeasurably increases the power of 'inter-learning', i.e. of learning from the experiences of others, whether near or distant in time or space. It is clearly this change which makes human development distinctively social development. The development or fulfilment of human potentialities through tradition, mutual stimulus, selection, and co-operation proceeds chiefly by means of those changes in the relations between individuals which constitute social structure.'[1]

---

[1] Ginsberg, *Reason and Unreason in Society*, p. 29.

XI

DEMOCRATIC POLITICAL THEORY: APPLICATIONS

(a) *Democracy: the test*

WHERE, we may now ask, has our search for the foundations of a democratic political theory led us? We have sought them in the analysis not of the cosmos but of human life and behaviour, by discussing purpose in man not in the universe. Our aim, too, has not been prophecy but practical guidance. As to the future the result is not coloured by that optimism which has characterized so large a part of the advocacy of democracy. For our argument makes no claim that rightness necessarily belongs to majority decisions. Nor does it rely on the belief that truth, given democratic freedoms, must prevail. There lies behind it no evolutionistic assumption of inevitable progress. It is a stranger to the metaphysical notion that the voice of the people is the voice of God, or that there is a providential ordering of human history expressing itself either in the cumulative wisdom of social tradition or the individual inspiration of the inner light, and by one means or another shaping our ends 'rough-hew them how we will'. On the other hand, our thesis does not accept the view that there is a necessary levity or ignorance in democracy which ensures that it shall be succeeded by despotism as the next stage in an inevitable cycle of change. Rather would it argue, with Mill, that wisdom has a greater prospect of prevailing where there is free and open discussion and error can be confuted by argument; even though it agreed, with those who stress the influence of economic conditions and interests on the formulation of ideas, that such a prospect is enhanced by greater social equality and, conversely, is reduced where privilege distorts the interpretation of the social good.

But if no claim is made for the sanctity of the majority, or of special kinds of minority, it is made for the fundamental importance of the principle that human purpose lies for each in the conscious direction of life to accord with his ordered experience. Although such harmony and integration are never absolute or complete in achievement, and there is only a more or less of them, and no system of government can guarantee them, their implication is essentially democratic. That principle is opposed, by definition, to all authoritarianism because it denies the premiss of special right or privilege. Essentially it is in line with democracy because the process by which decision is reached in democracy is that of open discussion with freedom to all to produce evidence and argument and come to what conclusion they will. This is the submission of the action of all to the judgment of all. Indeed, the very keynote of the democratic scheme is conformity of social action with the widest possible consciousness of purpose. The essence of the democratic method lies not in the counting of heads but in the submission of everything to discussion in which each has an equal right to state his case and an equal duty, in his own as well as in the social interest, to contribute his judgment. Its aim is a consensus; but if that is the ideal, where it is not reached and there is a need for decision the only practical procedure is to find the majority view, as that which has the least bad effects because it will offend the fewest.

Now this submission to discussion has several consequences profoundly significant in their tendency to contribute to social purpose as here defined. It encourages, because it relies upon, the articulation of all ideas in as generally comprehensible terms as possible, bringing them into the field of social consciousness. It subjects them to tests of the reasonable culled from cumulative experience, and thus enlarges the rational element contained in social ideals and policies. It leads to adjustment or compromise because the debate is never closed, thus tending to bring about the adaptation of ideas to changes in knowledge and experience, or differences in their interpretation. It promotes the integration of ideas by bringing them out into open juxtaposition. Although conflict may not be removed by this, it is a mistake to suppose that it is enhanced by being expressed.

For it is in these things that the virtue of democracy lies, not in any sacred authority belonging to majorities. How strange is the compliment paid by the modern dictator to this false definition of democracy. And how entirely empty of content in any way derived from the real essence of democracy. While plebiscitary dictatorship is readily recognized as having only a superficial resemblance to democracy, the reason why it has no significance in terms of the basic principles to which government by discussion is a response lies at the heart of political theory, and is not so easily seen. For they postulate active consent. They imply political responsibility as not a spasmodic but a continuous process, in the sense that authority must explain and justify itself in relation to all its acts, and aim at a constant renewal of confidence. Clearly the objective of maximizing conscious control of activity carries the implication of continuity in the reference of action to purpose. Authority is defined in terms of social function rather than of persons. It is the power granted to do certain determinate things or to use the force necessary to fulfil certain prescribed tasks. It is thus concerned with the performance of purpose that can be traced back to the minds of others, that belongs not to the agent but to society.

No form of government other than democracy leads to this reference back to the purposes of all, generalized through discussion into the nearest approach practically possible to a common denominator, and tested by criteria of rationality. That is by no means to assert that the rationality of decision arrived at through free discussion cannot be exaggerated. The demagogue may carry to a fine art the appeal to emotion, and convert reasoning men into a herd blindly following him, abdicating their judgment in favour of an 'inspired' leader. By playing upon hatred or fear, skilfully using psychological inhibitions or frustrations, and unscrupulously making even the intellectual or moral assumptions of the masses into a basis for false conclusions, the master of propaganda can sometimes mould the will of the multitude, even while acknowledging the lying unreality of what he is making them accept and the evil that he is persuading them to do. Not only did Hitler openly express his belief that the big lie would often succeed where the little lie would not; but he wrote in *Mein Kampf* that 'the masses feel very little shame at being terrorised intellectually and are scarcely conscious of the fact that their freedom as human beings is being impudently abused'.

This serves to make it all the clearer that there is no presumption of rationality about majority, or public, or mass opinion. Monarchies and aristocracies have often enough shown themselves blind and wrong-headed to preclude also any such claim for them. And there is no reason to suppose anything different of class or party dictatorships emerging in modern conditions. On the other hand, the protagonists for the might of propaganda, and the easy victory of emotion over reason, exaggerate their case. They have not enough belief in it themselves to make them willing to rely on it once they have achieved power. Nor did such practitioners of the art as the Nazis, Fascists, or Bolsheviks gain control of the state by its means alone; still less retain it. Clearly there are salutary tests of the reasonable which operate where discussion is free and which its enemies cannot afford to allow. Authority, whether it take the form of a dictator, a popular majority, or anything else, inasmuch as it restricts the free expression of opinion, diminishes the prospect both of discovering the most reasonable course—or, as Mill put it, of exchanging truth for error—and of reflecting the experience and will of the public.

Nor is there any presumption in favour of any particular minority that it possesses a monopoly of the truth, or even can be relied on for a probably greater degree of wisdom. Yet it seems to be one of the invariable accompaniments of the assertion of an objective morality to claim that some more or less definite body of the 'elect' or the specially trained are its natural guardians and interpreters. This body differs according to the nature of the doctrine; history shows many examples. It need not be a Pope, Calvin, group of church elders, or even congregation of the 'saved'. It may be a Comtist academy producing a 'scientific' pattern of the good. Or the voice of predestined history may be deemed to speak through a party which has won mastery of the state. The leaders of the working class may be held to have replaced the bourgeoisie, just as the middle class industrial entrepreneurs were thought to have supplanted a leisured and landed aristocracy, as the recipients of grace, the men who tread in 'the foremost files of time'. Disillusion is the invariable lot of such optimists.

(b) Democracy and the Moral Imperative

Most students of politics today would be rightly suspicious of any such view that it is the function of political science to show that the majority is right in its values because it is the majority, or a minority because of its special nature. Few, however, would dispute that it is concerned with the consequences in the behaviour of a society of accepting one set of values rather than another, such as sectional privilege or equality of claim, for clearly it deals with the description and analysis of particular kinds of political society. It may make generalizations which are based on observed behaviour—for example, that power corrupts and that there is an advantage in establishing checks on it, that independence of the judiciary is a condition of impartial judgment, that sovereignty increases the probability of war, that political reasoning is apt to be influenced by economic interests, that community requires certain common interests, beliefs, traditions, experiences, or institutions. It can examine the 'arrangement' or 'machinery' of political societies, point to the working of cause and effect within them, and so provide material for recommending how a desired objective is most likely to be achieved. Here, to repeat, it is based on observed behaviour and analysis of this, which may lead it into examination of human nature and its needs.

Aside from this descriptive and analytic function of political science, however, there is apt to be confusion or disagreement. Is it concerned with questions of 'ought', of what the state should do, of what are the obligations of the citizen, with rights and duties? Recently there has been a tendency, in order to establish its status as a science, to aver that, being a science, it can have nothing to do with values, that it cannot describe objectives but at the most, once objectives have been decided, can then indicate ways and means of attaining them. And there is the tendency also to assert, as we saw when discussing 'foundations and criteria' in Chapter II, that we cannot say anything useful about objectives because these are too vague, commonplace, or uncertain. Here however we have rejected this abdication and have claimed that what the state should aim at is the very essence of political studies.

To attempt to provide a basis for this claim and to find a solution for this problem it is best to start with what is agreed:

that political science is built upon the facts of human nature which include the needs that behaviour reveals as forming part of it. But any such analysis immediately shows that man is a purposive creature, having the distinctive characteristic of consciously directing his activities, and consciously exercising choice over the ends he pursues, and needing and demanding the freedom to do so. His needs must first comprehend, it is true, the satisfaction of bare physical necessities and the reasonably secure fulfilment of established expectations. He requires to develop habits that will economize the effort necessary to organize his daily life and, by establishing routines, free the mind from too many petty preoccupations; he needs change and variety too, the refreshment and stimulation of escape from routines—a satisfying adjustment between these opposites of stability and adventure. His activity must have a creative element capable of producing a sense of achievement. He needs to matter to others, to enjoy some measure of affection and sympathy, to satisfy the craving to 'belong' to family, friends, the group, and to bring his influence to bear upon them. Having aesthetic sensibilities, he must meet them through art, music, drama, literature. But what he requires also is something which co-ordinates these satisfactions, a consciousness that they are welded together into a pattern interpreting them, fitting them into a scheme of priorities adjusted to external circumstance and individual uniqueness—a pattern which he approves and which, because he approves it, may be said to express a personal *weltanschauung* and to provide a personal fulfilment. They are not enjoyments that 'happen anyhow'. Each has his values which he seeks to reflect in his behaviour. He is aware of the needs and more or less consciously develops a pattern of life designed to satisfy them. For he gives priorities to these satisfactions, that is to say he attaches more or less importance to them, treating some as 'better' than others. He forms an idea of the good and acts in accordance with it: or, at least, there is discernible from his course of conduct a more or less consistent pattern of values. It is true that he may not always admit this, but may say rather that he frequently knows good and does evil, but in that case it is no less clear that he makes this moral distinction. Moral consciousness, that is to say, is a fundamental part of his nature.

M

But so also, it may well be said, is inconsistency. He sets himself aims which he cannot achieve. Or he professes aims with his tongue which his conduct shows he is not in fact seeking. He fails to adjust his conscious pattern of values to the course of life his experience proves to give him most satisfaction, or to adjust his course of life to this conscious pattern. Such maladjustment is certainly so regular a fact, though in varying degree, as to require to be treated as a normal state of affairs. Its variation is one of the uncertainties in the material with which political science has to deal.

But political science cannot be satisfied with looking exclusively at one or the other. It would perhaps be safer to deduce the pattern of ideals from the behaviour rather than the reverse, but neither is fully intelligible or corrected until checked by the other. A man's aims may often be better gauged from what he does than from his own account of them, but often also his acts can only be understood by reference to his aims. In any case, however, the fact is that he exercises choice, and this choice implies preferences, values, a pattern, whether this is clearly conceived by himself or not, and whether or not it is a correct interpretation of his behaviour, or consistent with itself.

Were it not so, did he not exercise choice on a judgment of values, but react automatically to his environment, it would only be necessary to examine his environment to produce from it laws or generalizations—in which there could certainly be no content of values. And political science would be like natural science, descriptive, and 'exact'. What hinges it to values is the fact that men's behaviour is hinged to values. To understand the one is impossible without studying the other. That is why it is true to say that politics is subordinate to ethics. That he makes a judgment of good and evil, and aims at acting in accordance with it, makes it his purpose, distinguishes man and is as much a part of human nature as weight is of substance. Thus political science cannot escape this fact. It is concerned with 'ought' because man is, and it is a study of man. It has to take his ideas of 'ought' as it finds them because these influence, if not determine, his actions in political society, and the nature and actions of political society itself cannot be explained apart from them.

And all that we thus predicate to man we must predicate to society also. It too is purposive. That is not to claim that we can, or need to, point to any particular moment at which its purposes were laid down, or that they were ever delimited by an identifiable act. Some communities, it is true, have come nearer than others to articulating their purposes as they conceived them at some specific time. But declarations of independence or of the rights of man are no more than incidents momentarily crystallising a political faith in a form which contemporary circumstance dictates. They certainly indicate social purpose as this is agreed at that instant and expressed in what is necessarily an incomplete, and probably in some measure a transient, form. We do not depend upon them, however, for the predication of purpose to the state. We do not have to show that the state was created to achieve some particular thing in order to deny that it is an incomprehensible phenomenon to be accepted without questioning its use or aim. Because this use and aim is not always articulated it is not the less self-evident that it exists. Since the state clearly serves some of the purposes of its members we are concerned with its relevance to them. It has purpose because they have purposes and give it purpose.

Thus far there seems to be at least widespread agreement. Disagreement arises rather over the further question, whether it is possible to discover principles or laws governing what man's purposes ought to be, and whether political study is concerned with this. Can it deduce from physics, biology, metaphysics, or history, or a combination of them, laws of the universe with which it ought to be man's business to conform? Is it concerned with a criterion over and above the moral ideas men actually cherish, by which these can be tested, an 'ought' behind the several ideas of 'ought'? Such laws imply a purpose behind and above that of man. They either determine the latter automatically, in which case there is no freedom of choice and no problem, since what is must be and what must be is. Or they constitute an ideal end which it is man's moral duty to pursue, and they thus indicate the objective which any society, including the state, ought to make its own. If such laws exist and are discoverable there is no doubt that they must delimit political science. Such, indeed, was the claim, for instance, of the theocratic reaction to the French Revolution. Laying down human purpose, they command the political scientist to examine how it can best be realized and to translate it into political institutions. For that reason it seems difficult to deny that it is incumbent upon him to examine the case made by various philosophies for the existence of such laws, and indeed their claims to have discovered them. The view here taken, however, is that the case is unproved and the claims without substance. And if the view is accepted political science ceases to be concerned with the 'ought' behind the 'ought', and deals only with man's moral ideas as explanations of, and in relation to, their behaviour—as it finds them. It takes them, that is to say, as part of the facts it has to work with. It describes them as it finds them and examines their implications in terms of political organization. It deals with their practical consequences.

But it is concerned to explain them too, which is to say that it seeks to discover how they arise, and to analyse the interpretation they express. And at this point political theory does more than describe: it appraises. For it considers how far ideas—and the institutions in which they are expressed—meet the needs they are an endeavour to satisfy. It therefore suggests judgments about their reasonableness. It may compare different precepts for their coherence, and their consistency with experience. Varying practices and arrangements may be tested by their results. Thus it may produce reasons for preferring one set of ideas, institutions, or machinery to another; but those reasons will take the form of arguing that they better secure the satisfaction of human needs and the realization of human ends, not that they more closely conform to an *a priori* first principle, such as evolutionary necessity or the dialectic of history, laid down by extra-human agency. The 'ought' they imply will thus be, as it were, a common 'ought', a quintessential 'ought', expressing an attempt at the most rational interpretation of experience, not an 'ought' behind experience dictating conclusions regardless of it.

How far does another contention affect this position, namely that conduct is to be justified not in terms of ideas rationally conceived, but of emotions such as fear, envy, greed, love or hatred? Man is a miserable being anxious only for self-preservation. Or, man is never so truly great as when he acts from his passions. The answer is that while ideas affecting conduct seem often to be arrived at by a process which it is impossible to say is either completely rational or completely

DEMOCRATIC POLITICAL THEORY: APPLICATIONS 181

emotional, nonetheless the more emotion and passion are canalized by the rational element in man, the more emotional force is directed by mental activity, the greater is the prospect of the good life and of happiness, because the more will it be adapted to reality and express the conscious control of circumstance.

Now in making such calculations political science is bound to accept the fact that the *weltanschauung* of many people is built upon the belief in just such an absolute or revealed concept as here has been criticized as baseless or unproved. It can scarcely deny that morality for such must consist in compliance with its commands. But in no way is the political scientist precluded from commenting upon it. He may point out, for instance, that its claim is not in fact accorded the universal acceptance implicit in its assertion of finality, and that this question of acceptance is what in the first place concerns him as a political scientist. For his grant to the believer in it of the right to act upon it, and the duty to do so, carries with it the corollary that the unbeliever has also the right to act on his unbelief.

In the second place, he is entitled—indeed, it is his job—as a political scientist to consider and suggest how far a particular *weltanschauung* would appear to cover the facts, to meet basic needs, to be compatible with social life, to have internal self-consistency, to be really conducive to self-realization. Although he cannot claim that any finality attaches to his judgment, he is especially concerned to examine the consequences of applying it, and in doing so to draw conclusions about how far it can be expected to contribute to or stand in the way of the general development of rational control over environment and activity therein. He cannot say that the Sermon on the Mount or a doctrine of race hegemony is good or true—although as a philosopher or historian he may have views on such questions—but he can examine the effects of each on individuals and on society, and in doing so he will make judgments in terms of such ends as happiness and the good life, which men verbally or by their behaviour profess.

So it may be said that political theory starts from the facts of moral consciousness. Men require a system of social co-operation wherein to satisfy their needs. They seek in this system a pattern of institutions which reflects their moral ideas and makes possible a way of life which is in harmony with them. What is required of that pattern in order that it shall do this is the direct concern of political science. How, it has to consider, does the state need to be organized so that such moral fulfilment shall be rendered possible.

(c) *Rights and Duties*

By contrast, preoccupation with the state as a sovereign body, or as the incarnation of social morality, leads, as a counterweight, to the insistent emphasis on rights which, if they are to be regarded as limitations on its authority, must have an equally absolute character. 'Natural' omnipotence is opposed by 'natural' rights to the non-exercise of omnipotence. Historically this treatment is easily explained. Political power has greatly accumulated during recent centuries in the growth of the nation-state with its much more efficient instruments of compulsion. It has therefore become all the more necessary for power to be studied, explained, justified and the limits to it, if any, defined. But if it has grown, so also has the social consciousness developed; so too has the growth of scientific knowledge increased awareness of the possibilities of controlling environment. From accepting the position of being a victim of power the citizen seeks to become its master and to use it for his own ends. Consequently, when confronted by leviathan, the political theorist imbued with a liberal humanism lays all the greater emphasis on, and draws all the wider his definition of, rights as a counterblast to its claims.

On the other hand, to see the state not as a leviathan but as merely an association for the achievement of agreed ends is to invite consideration of the methods and systems of co-operation by which societies arrange their affairs, and discussion of them in terms of the ends they seek to serve. Thus the rights and obligations both of the members and of the association are seen as terms of the process of co-operation, or as necessary aspects of the institutions in which it expresses itself.

The obligations of the citizen can now be looked at more closely in their social context. While his general obligation is to develop and apply his personal moral ideal, this involves the recognition of an identical need in all other citizens. And this recognition may be said to imply three particular obligations. The first of these is to promote the good life in others, as the counterpart of his own need, by encouraging and assisting in them the growth of knowledge, wide experience, the free exercise of judgment, the development of rational processes of thought. It means that he must not deny them the freedom to experiment. Still less may he restrain their enjoyment of opportinities which he claims for himself. He has the duty to tolerate whatever conclusions the experience of others may lead them to draw, although he has also the duty to contribute his own informed judgment to the pool from which they can derive the lessons of a wider experience than their own. It is an obligation to encourage, to persuade, to warn, but above all to promote the free exercise of reason in interpreting experience and understanding the world, by means of reasoned as opposed to imperative statement, to teach rather than to command.

The second obligation arises from the necessary division of labour in every society, whether small like the family or large like the nation. It is to contribute by production and service to the means whereby the good life can be led. Just as ideas, knowledge, understanding and judgment provide the mental activity on which the good life depends, so does it also depend on physical conditions which are the artificial product of labour and skill. And to contribute these according to individual ability and social need is a reciprocal obligation attaching to all members of society as the corollary of its purpose because this requires them for its achievement. It is possible, of course, to consider in detail the varying practical interpretations which may be given to this principle; for the moment it is enough to point out that it exists.

Thirdly, there is what might be called the obligation to show a co-operative disposition toward the institutions of the society whose membership the citizen has accepted, and in whose life— with its merits, its advantages to him, and its defects—he participates. Since co-operation is not the same thing as conformity there are times when it may be better expressed by reasoned disagreement aimed at improvement than by inert acceptance; where the opportunity for reasoned disagreement is denied, co-operation may even carry the paradoxical implication of a duty to disobey. Resistance, both passive and active, has been proclaimed a right in some circumstances, or even a supreme obligation, by many of the leading figures of political thought in all ages. And those citizens whose principles have led them into it—like John Knox, Hampden, Cromwell, Washington, Garibaldi, Gandhi—have not seldom earned the gratitude and admiration of posterity. There is clearly a point too at which tyranny, having left no other avenue of escape, must submit to the very arbitrament of force which it has itself erected. Had Adolf Hitler been assassinated, few today surely would condemn the violence; on the contrary many would regard the deed as a praiseworthy act of liberation and him who was responsible for it as the truest contributor to the good of society. Thus resistance or violence directed against forces which are obstructive to social good may be in some circumstances the best way of co-operating in the life of society.

But in the conditions of a modern democracy the idea of a co-operative disposition may be allowed to have a much more constructive application than that. The citizen cannot escape some share of responsibility for the way in which his society is run. He clearly has an obligation to do all in his power to see that this is improved. While the more do positive law and social conventions coincide with his personal conviction of right the firmer is his duty to obey them, where they do not he should make the fullest use of the opportunities which social and political institutions make available to him in order to get them changed. The greater his freedom in this respect, the weaker must be his moral claim to the right of nonconformity, and the larger his personal responsibility for the prevailing system. His obligation to obey can never, it is true, be absolute or complete, but where he is in some doubt—still more, where the matter is of little importance—the duty to be co-operative implies giving the benefit of the doubt to society, giving full weight to the advantages of avoiding disturbance of a settled way of doing things and to the disadvantages of offending persons and upsetting habits, and risking a bigger evil for the sake of a smaller good. This is not to say, as some have done, that the citizen should distrust his reason, but that, humble in his claims to its having reached any finality, and striving always to make it as comprehensive as possible, he should yet be determined to uphold it against the open attacks of unreason and the more insidious ones of compromise. To venerate where we are unable presently to comprehend is no more likely to lead to saintly humility or scientific openness of mind than to a servile acceptance of abuses and an unwillingness to contemplate—let alone to seek—improvements. Nor is this to extol Morley's conservative with his pygmy hope that some day things may be better shivering beside his giant conviction that they might be infinitely worse.

Alongside such obligations of the citizen are his 'rights', or what may be better called the duties of the state to its members. Of these three things may be said in general. They are determined basically by the purpose of society itself. They are governed, that is to say, by the same considerations as are the obligation of the citizen: to encourage and promote the good life, the realization of the self, or the fulfilment of the personality, of one and all. That does not imply, it is true, as Hobhouse points out, that any self or any development of personality, regardless of its nature, is to be regarded as equally good. It does not deny the existence of scales of preference, although it does question the possibility of finding any more objective test that one is better than another, than can be derived from the fact that the more rational it is—the more, that is, it takes account of in experience and weaves into a consistent whole—the more is it worthy of respect and the stronger is its claim to freedom of application. It is built upon the recognition of the uniqueness of experience and is dubious of any assertion that an objective scale of universal application has been finally discovered, that would justify the establishment of a pattern of behaviour generally valid—the universality of its applicability depending upon the universality of acceptance of the moral concept it embodies.

The second general point about rights is their identity in all citizens. Each has an equal claim upon society; or the duties of society are directed towards the good of all in equal measure, giving favour or privilege to none. This would be so even if only for the negative reason that none can prove a better claim to the opportunity to lead the good life than another. And the most that the state can do is to secure the opportunity; it cannot ensure that this will be used. But it may also be argued that since the purpose of society is the purpose of its members and is defined thereby, it cannot be the purpose of some of its members as any exclusiveness would imply. Or, to turn from the subject of purpose to its object, again the good life being no more desirable for one than another, there is no justification for making it more possible to one than another. On the other hand, there is no incompatibility with this argument in admitting that the duty of the state so defined implies that either of two circumstances justifies the varying of help socially given towards the good life. The first is evidence of varying need and capacity. The second is evidence of varying ability to contribute by service to the good of others.

Thirdly, individual rights or social duties are thus seen as the recognition of proper relationships in society. They are a way of expressing the conditions in which a society seems most likely to achieve its purpose. In this fashion they are, as it were, innate in society and 'natural' in that sense rather than 'natural' to man over against society. They are the creation neither of man nor of society, but terms of the process of co-operation by which the ends of both are realized.

In such an attempt to consider moral concepts for their bearing upon political theory we may say, then that we make three assumptions. The first is that of equality. Man being the end in himself, his good is the ultimate end which society serves; and no man has a greater claim than any other that his good should have priority. The second is that of obligation on the part of each to his personal ideal. For his personal ideal represents his judgment of that way of life which is on the whole good, which therefore he desires, and the requirements of which he regards as obligatory upon him. The third is that self-satisfaction comes through the fulfilment of such obligations. This is not only because ideals 'are related to and arise from fundamental human needs'[1] but because the justification of the personal moral ideal is that it is designed to satisfy the needs of which the self is conscious. Indeed, although it may, and often does, 'tend to transform them and control them' in the process of satisfying them, unless it does satisfy these needs it will require modification. Or, put in another way, the personal moral ideal being 'the objective counterpart of the self which, as self-conscious, is a unity . . . the realization of the goods which in

[1] Ginsberg, 'Basic Needs and Moral Ideals,' p. 198, *Proceedings of the Aristotelian Society, 1948–9*.

their inter-relation constitute the moral ideal involves the realization of the self.'[1] Or again, 'in doing what he believes to be required by his ideal, the individual always achieves the realization and expression of his moral personality. . . . While the actual ends at which an individual aims may not be achieved, his greatest good, the expression of his moral personality and the development of his character, is always achieved in the pursuit.'[2]

(d) *Rights as Elements in Social Purpose*

Apart from such general considerations, rights may be examined as the specific claims which have entered into the political discussions of recent centuries. What can be said about the rights to life, liberty and property, which have been for long so familiar an expression in Anglo-American political thinking as to have seemed to achieve the status of political axioms?

Life is obviously so basic a condition of all else that the first question is whether there can ever be a justification for denying the right to it. In one sense there cannot, for the denial excludes all possibility of achieving the purpose of society so far at least as concerns the person involved, and means instead the final abandonment of such purpose. For that reason it is difficult to see that it can ever be justified as consistent with the fundamental assumptions of the political association itself. The most that can be said is that it may sometimes be expedient as a means practically necessary to prevent an even worse failure, the loss of yet more life or of yet more possibility of achieving the good life. It is a right, that is to say, limited by the need to defend the conditions on which the good life for all depends. The state has the overriding duty to meet that need. This means first that it must not countenance the sacrifice of life except as a last resort when it has exhausted every other means of performing its task. It means, secondly, that it has the duty to organize the defence of society. And just as the individual cannot deny his obligation to do the right as he sees it under the threat of violence, so must the association recognize that obligation. Inasmuch as the way of life which it deems good and its own freedom to apply it are

[1] Macbeath, *Experiments in Living* (1952), p. 418.
[2] *Ibid.*, p. 48.

threatened by force it must organize force to resist the threat. The loss of life which this entails is an evil, but it may be an unavoidable evil, about which all that can be done is to ensure that it is kept to a minimum.

When we turn to the second member of the trilogy we are faced by a different order of difficulty, that of definition. What do we mean by liberty? The disadvantage in insisting on freedom as an end arises first from the fact that it is essentially a negative idea—meaning the absence of restraint—and there are practical objections to the notion of pursuing a negative. The second and even greater disadvantage lies in its extreme vagueness. This may strengthen its use as a battle-cry, since each may include in it whatever particular absence of restraint he most favours. But in order that it shall serve as a measure for practical policies it must be given much greater precision, and the process of rendering it more precise inevitably opens the way to many kinds of disagreement.

So in any discussion of the right to liberty the first point to be clear about is the way in which we are using the term. To treat it as the absence of restraint is negative but it has the advantage of corresponding more closely to everyday usage. The attempts made to define it in a positive sense, as meaning obedience to the law or to certain kinds of law, lead only to confusion for they end by equating liberty with constraint. To say that a man is being forced to be free when he is in fact being prevented from doing what he wants, or being compelled to do what society wants, is to give the term an alien content, stretching it to mean something for which other terms should be found. The treatment of liberty as an abstract concept with an absolute meaning can be explained historically as meeting the need for an instrument to counter the claims of state absolutism. It is only a hindrance where political society is regarded as an essay in co-operation. For then what is needed is to consider not liberty in a vague and general way but in relation to specific practical activities, as liberty to think, to speak, to meet, to move, to associate, to work, to be educated, to obtain the economic means of livelihood, and so on. It is given a positive content in this way. It can be seen, moreover, as corresponding to duties on the part of the state to organize conditions favourable to the achievement of the purpose for which it exists.

Necessary liberties are the means necessary to the good life.

Clearly thinkers in the liberal tradition have understood liberty broadly in this way, at least from Mill to Laski. Mill's claim was essentially that there must be the greatest possible freedom of experience, and for every process of learning from one's own experience and that of others. Laski always makes the assumption that man in seeking his happiness achieves it by following the teaching of his 'unique' experience. Freedom is thought of as necessary for the achievement of happiness in the sense that a class deprived of access to power will be denied the conditions of happiness; because a privileged group tends to equate social good with its own. But this is not the same as the defence of freedom in Mill's sense because even if such were not the case, and the privileged group used its power selflessly to promote the social good, as may perhaps be claimed at some times to have happened, it still would not be creating the greatest amount of self-realization. For this, as we have argued, is not constituted by satisfaction of a list of wants. Liberty, as constituted by the institutions of free elective government, is necessary to happiness not only because it is a means of guaranteeing the recognition by the state of the needs of its citizens in the priority in which they are felt, but also because it is the condition for giving meaning and purpose to activity, itself a condition of self-realization. For the greater the freedom of experience, of reflection thereon, leading to life in accordance with that reflection, the greater the potentiality of self-realization and happiness. For only action willed by the self can contribute to self-realization. If the experience of its consequences does not accord with expectations the effect will be to modify reason and will; but unless that adjustment springs from experience, or from active acceptance by the reason of the lessons of others' experience, which is indirect experience, it cannot constitute a real alteration of will; and action not the result of such an alteration can only be the result of an additional external compulsion without meaning for self-development. Liberty not only is necessary to self-realization, but a part of the price that has to be paid for it is the making of mistakes. Freedom to make a wrong judgment—wrong in that its consequences are not correctly anticipated—is the pre-condition of ability to make a right judgment. By attempting to prevent what it regards, rightly or wrongly, as the making of a mistaken judgment authority may be preventing the achievement of rational judgment and discouraging the making of any judgment at all, thus hindering the growth of morality. Instead it should be actively promoting this by encouraging freedom of thought and experiment, and the pooling of knowledge and the opportunities of learning. Only when it is clear that such learning cannot take place from experience—because, for instance, the result would be fatal—can it be justifiably prevented. But authority is then preventing for the same reason as it is otherwise encouraging and assisting, namely on the principle that self-realization is the purpose it serves.

What also of the case where a man's free choice leads him to abandon freedom, saying that he prefers to yield his conscience to the keeping of church or state, that he wants to be constrained, to be told what to do, that he has more faith in others than in himself? Clearly it cannot then be said that authority is increasing happiness by denying him this freedom to follow, to imitate, to resign his judgment and obey. For that is what he wants to do, and we have to accept his statement that in this abdication he finds happiness. But again we can claim that authority should intervene at the point where this abandonment of freedom is so complete as to remove the possibility of its ever being regained. On the principle that self-realization is the purpose it serves authority may permit him so to yield his judgment, but on the same principle it must ensure both that he is in a position to reassert it and that he is not denied the material to encourage such reassertion.

Very similar considerations apply to discussions of the right to property as apply to liberty. Indeed the reason for giving special distinction to the former is more historical than logical. For it means the liberty to appropriate for immediate use or to acquire and keep for future use, and so is parallel with the right to sustenance, shelter, education or such other things as are necessary to the maintenance of life. It demands particular attention, however, because it can be so differently interpreted. Man clearly has a basic need to appropriate certain things to himself—food, for example. As Locke pointed out, it must have become his at some moment, whether when he digested, cooked or culled it. Man clearly has a basic need, too, for such personal belongings as clothes, furniture, the decorations of his person and home, the tools of his trade, the instruments of his comfort, culture and amusement. He also needs security of the kind that comes from saving or storing the means of future satisfaction. No serious social problems are raised by allowing him the satisfaction of such needs; so that property in such things can be reasonably admitted. At the other end of the scale is property in persons. No one would defend the institution of slavery today although it was regarded, even comparatively recently among some civilized nations, as a permissible embodiment of property rights. But, being the antithesis of self-realization, no society which recognizes that as its purpose can countenance it. Somewhere between these extremes must come the other forms of property. To own his home and some land around it are able to give a man enduring pleasure and to satisfy in him a need which many feel. The same may be true of a business enterprise, such as a factory, farm, shop or coal-mine. In both cases it may well be that ownership encourages a sense of personal responsibility leading to creative endeavour and social advantage. It may also mean, however, that one or a few are enabled to exercise power over the lives of others because they control the instruments necessary for them to be able to produce.

Thus property is seen as a term, like liberty, having such a wide meaning that it cannot be usefully considered in a general way. It can take some forms which are clearly admissible and others which are as clearly inadmissible. Only when it is given a more precise meaning, such as property in clothes or in coal-mines, property in the house one lives in or the houses that others live in, can it be fruitfully discussed. As a right it is not absolute but relative to the contribution it makes to the purpose of society. Its boundaries can only be drawn empirically. It is evident that each additional possession represents for its owner a further liberty for self-expression, a further opportunity of control over his environment, while for others it may constitute a privation. To own one's own home offers the chance of satisfactions of a different order and of a more direct and continuing kind than to own the homes of other people. Happiness may be derived from a sense of security and permanence, and also from the knowledge that it may be given or bequeathed to one who too may have expressed his or her personality in its creation or embellishment. In addition there may be social advantage in encouraging the care which such ownership promotes. But while it is obvious that the secured possession of certain objects may be an essential means to the fulfilment of individual personality, there are others where private ownership may stand in the way of such fulfilment because of the degree of power it implies over the daily lives of others. Collective ownership of a large industrial enterprise, for instance, inasmuch as it promotes co-operative control by those engaged in it creates a wider field for their conscious direction of their own activities. In addition it may be that the enterprise is of such importance to the life of society that society as a whole needs to determine its operations. Consequently there may be a strong case for here drawing the line limiting the right to private property in favour of public property. But the social purpose of maximum control, conscious and direct, of conditions and way of life remains the ultimate test.

Consideration of the right to property leads naturally to what might be called the right to welfare services. A man needs to provide for his maintenance and care should unemployment, ill-health or old age render him unable to earn a living. One method of meeting such needs is through a system of private property designed to secure individual savings, competitive insurance, and accumulations of privately owned realizable capital. Another is through the social provision of welfare services. The efficiency with which one or the other meets the needs can be judged by results. Each in fact shows the recognition of such a right as a term of the processes of social co-operation, the latter far more clearly and directly than the former. But since these needs are obvious, defenders of the former system have always in fact to argue that it provided for their satisfaction. Indeed, these needs being fundamental the social machinery designed to supply them is a basic part of the system of co-operation which the state represents.

Similarly the right to education is another way of expressing the duty implicit in the state to secure educational opportunity to every citizen. Like maintenance in sickness and old age it is a necessary corollary of the definition of purpose, the conditions for the good life for all, which has been put forward as attaching to the state. Being an essential and obvious part of those conditions there is no room for doubt as to the right itself, although there may be variations in the possible methods of satisfying it. And on these there can be no final judgment on grounds of principle but only an empirical answer in terms of practical efficacy. But practical efficacy will itself have to be judged by the same criterion of social purpose: the question has to be asked of it, that is, how far it helps and encourages rational valuation by showing its relation to experience and its application in intelligent behaviour.

Indeed, we are here very near to the heart of that doctrine. For what it is the purpose of men to use the state to secure, it must also be their purpose to teach the child. The good life which is the object of that state must be the object of education too. When it was held that this depended on the acceptance of a discipline based on a revelation and imposed by authority, then the primary function of education was to teach and enforce the dogma and inculcate compatible habits of mind and conduct. Subservience to accepted truth was then its end and discipline its means. Because that is, indeed, still a widely held view of the basis of the good life, though much less so than in Victorian times, much of educational objectives and methods still follows that pattern. But its inadequacy is patent. Its effect is to divorce what goes on in school from life outside. Knowledge is not related to understanding the world as a living environment; its acquisition becomes a dead routine from which there is no satisfaction save in escape into reality. Learning loses its fascination of power achieved, and mental activity grows instead into a misery to avoid. There thus develops a natural contrast between behaviour in and out of school. That is the divorce of the classroom, with its rigid and disagreeable discipline, from the playground where all is chaos, noise, and an anarchy in which, as in the example cited by Leonard Woolf,[1] each gives uncontrolled vent to momentary impulse undirected to any end, and behaves without attempt at reasonable integration. This divorce, however, is the very denial of the primary function of education, of meeting the need for ordered understanding and for developing the mechanisms of intelligent behaviour—a function which can only be performed by the more difficult method, though in the long run probably the

[1] Cf. his discussion of education in *Principia Politica*.

smoother method, of relating what is taught to the child's own interest, of explaining precept by reference to its own experience, and so avoiding this divorce. This may well be the smoother method because, as it is what the child is himself seeking to do, it will the more readily enlist his active co-operation. Anyway it alone is in line with social purpose as here defined.

The authoritarian system is wrong because it is based on a wrong reading of human nature. This it postulates as evil—since the Fall from Grace—and therefore to be exorcised, hated, and suppressed by force. The truth is that it is better to teach by love and patience than by force and fear, or perhaps even that this is the only effective way of teaching at all. The point is that the former method teaches acceptance—for example, of principles of conduct—as a free act of the intelligence, thus incorporating them into mental activity. It is best if they are so incorporated because they are intelligently seen to be reasonable on the basis of judgments of the results experienced, for that is the most enduring test. But it is true that acceptance may also be given because it wins the satisfaction of approval where approval is sought and desired.

The conclusion is, then, that education must aim to lead the child to incorporate voluntarily the facts of his experience and to learn how to build an intelligent valuation by rationally integrating them. He is doing this when he builds from his own direct experience, but a preliminary part of the process will often be to follow freely the example of someone he respects who has a wider knowledge. He may be doing this too when he carries out—or refrains from—an act because it will give pleasure—or pain—to someone he loves. But when he refrains because ordered not so to act or to avoid the pain of punishment that is quite a different thing: he has not in that case incorporated it into his pattern of the good; what he has then incorporated is the fear of punishment or the need for subservience to another's will; and so he has learnt nothing but to abdicate his moral responsibility of constructing the pattern of good. And it is then that the fundamental aim of education is defeated and its processes rendered destructive.

(e) *Political Studies*

The study of politics may be regarded as taking place, then,

DEMOCRATIC POLITICAL THEORY: APPLICATIONS 195

at two levels—of ends and of means. The former relate to basic needs and may be classified as physical, mental, and social. The need for physical satisfactions and comforts springs from the facts of bodily constitution with its requirements for maintenance in health. Were man no more than an animal, it would perhaps be possible to stop at this point. But he is marked by mental activity. He seeks to understand the world about him, and in embarking upon that intellectual adventure he develops beliefs about its nature; ideas of good and evil; and purpose which he expresses through the intelligent application of means to ends. So that if the second category of needs relates to mental activity, it is for what may be called personal development or self-realization and involves the concept of 'the good life'. The third are social, the need of other people, to give and receive affection, approval, mutual service, to have the sense of belonging and of significant participation in communal life.

At this level, then, politics is concerned to discover regularities in ends and in the needs from which they spring. At least in broad character these needs are universal: all men have them. But men have them differently, laying a varied stress upon the different elements in them; there is great variety in the interpretation of needs and the methods of satisfying them. Important regularities emerge, however, in the process of interpretation; for one thing, this being built upon individual experience, the greater the similarity of experience in different persons the greater the probability of similarity in interpretation among them. For another, it is a process in which reason is brought to bear upon experience in order first to explain it and then to control or mould it to purpose. That men recognize reason as the instrument with which they must work if they are to achieve their ends is as true of the primitive as of men in the twentieth century. When the former practises continence or indulges in saturnalia in order to promote the growth of his crops, or sprinkles water to induce rain, or consults signs or oracles before deciding on acts of policy, he is using his reasoning powers to explain the world about him and applying that explanation to gain his ends. The process is rational in that it is an attempt to establish an orderly pattern of causal relationships between phenomena, and to use this purposively. That the explanation now appears false and the use of it wasted effort does not alter this. So that we have in this use of reason another regularity. Of course the better the quality of the reasoning and the more adequate the explanation it evokes the greater are the possibilities of practical achievement. To understand the chemistry of the soil, substituting it for false beliefs which would now be called magic, is to increase the potential mastery of nature. To learn the point at which indulgence debilitates instead of enhancing vitality makes possible a more amply satisfying pattern of behaviour than is afforded by conventions and taboos. To discover the response of others to particular courses of conduct is to widen the scope of co-operation. Values built upon fuller comprehension of experience are more productive of fulfilment than those built on inhibitions or prejudices. Reason itself is an imperfect instrument, and must be admitted to be so, but it is the only one. History and current social activities provide material from which regularities can in fact be elicited, deriving from similarities in needs, experience, and the ideas in which they result.

Such examination of purposes and the manner in which they are developed and formulated provides a basis for political studies at their second level, that is of the conditions and processes of co-operation in groups or associations such as the state. There is no reason why this part of political science, which deals analytically with the institutions of government, their manner of working, and the political relationships of citizens, should not exist of its own right; but it can both illuminate and be helped by the parallel study of ends. Each in fact is liable to lose by being pursued in isolation.

At the second level, political science is concerned with the working of the institutions in which co-operation is organized. It examines the condition in which such arrangements work. It seeks to explain the forms they take, to test the efficiency with which they achieve results. It tries to discover causal relations within them, giving rise to regularities or justifying generalizations. It aims fundamentally, for example, at learning the conditions which make men willing to obey, thus establishing political order, or cause them to disobey, thus bringing about revolution.

This basic part of the subject is what is sometimes called the problem of leadership. But the question of the relationship between leader and follower is only another way of expressing the question of obedience of subject to ruler. Since men seek to apply their belief-pattern in their activity the quality of leadership is to express the beliefs which are latent in men in such a way as to unite them behind a common point of view in order to obtain their action in unison. It is to persuade, to carry conviction, to galvanize into united purpose. It is also to show the means to achievement. Indeed it is to give a clearer perception of belief, converting it into practical purpose by the very process of showing the way of application. The danger to be avoided in such an emphasis on the quality of leadership is too exclusive a concern with the element of leadership itself. This is indeed a modern reaction to the over-emphasis on the element of consent which can be found in earlier analysis. Both are really essential. The leader cannot lead where the follower will not follow. The mass of men are not mere tinder waiting to be ignited by the flame of the Hero. The history of man is more than the history of great men. The more thoughtful, the more educated, the more politically conscious men are, the greater is the importance of the element of consent among them. If democratic thought has tended in the past to overestimate the degree to which the active citizen body is politically developed in this sense—and this may be so because it was both more concerned with restricted electorates and confronted by less complexity in the problems of social action—it shows a tendency today, after witnessing the mass hysteria evoked by the propaganda methods of demagogues and dictatorships, to forget the element of consent altogether and treat leadership as though it were simply a force imposed from above upon inert masses. Rather is it the ability to convert the thoughts and feelings of the many into common purpose, to assist men to a consciousness that integrates their beliefs and activities both individually and socially. There is thus a two-way movement with, on the one hand, leadership evoking response; and, on the other, the needs and experiences, and their interpretation in beliefs, ideals and purposes, of men in society determining the conditions and limitations of that response. Both offer much material for the political scientist seeking to explain the nature and working of society. The leader neither creates nor maintains society single-handed; he is a part of the process of creation and maintenance, as much evoked by it as evoking it, as much influenced by it as influencing it, but having nevertheless a special part to play in the whole system of co-operation, which it represents.

The quality of that part, and therefore the value of his contribution, can only be judged by results. And on the most immediate plane, the judges of those results will necessarily be the members of the society themselves, using such criteria as the degree and durability of the satisfactions produced by the leadership. It is one merit of democratic forms of government that they provide institutional channels for the expression of this judgment, just as they do for the initial selection and continued conditioning of the leadership. On a longer-term plane it may be suggested that the test of value in leadership is to be sought in the degree to which it succeeds in building the common perception on the true and real in experience, and in adapting the means to the achievement of the purposes in which the common perception takes shape.

(f) Applied Democracy

Political institutions, as the more or less systematic expression of co-operation within a particular society, inevitably embody and develop its own special traditions, ideas, and values. To be properly understood they must be seen in that relationship. But any such particular society must not be thought of as being, as it were, an ultimate and irreducible element. Though it may often have a long history of independent existence, it may not. Changing ideas may affect its composition as well as its relationship with other societies; by conquest or confederation or union it may merge in a larger unit, or by applying a principle of self-determination divide into smaller units. Medieval christendom was a society in a manner that the Europe of the early twentieth century was not. The British Empire of 1880, though held together by power, was less of a society than the British Commonwealth of 1950. Modern political theory in England accepting the nation-state as a fixed datum was contemporary with an Italy and a Germany that were no more than geographical expressions.

This is important because it means that political study must

DEMOCRATIC POLITICAL THEORY: APPLICATIONS 199

not wear the blinkers set by the traditions of a simple community. It is inadequate if based on the acceptance of a predetermined statehood, if founded on the assumption of necessity as attaching to given states. True the most illuminating method of approach to understanding a particular society's political institutions will often be by examining the history, traditions, culture, and ideas of that society. Especially is this so if they have endured for long, and the society itself has a lengthy life as a distinct entity. But complete intellectual insularity is not enough. No social history is entirely self-sufficient or uninfluenced by ideas and events in the rest of the world.

Nor, if there are differences between sets of people, are there not also similarities. All societies share characteristics that are common to human beings, common values and purposes. It is just as possible, and sometimes more fruitful, to study these as it is to study their differences, what is common to a European as what distinguishes a Frenchman and a Dane, what is common to man as what differs between an American and an Englishman. It is these which provide criteria for the general testing of all institutions of no matter what society; and no matter what order of ideas, what religion, what system of custom or tradition may have grown up in the effort to meet these needs.

It follows from what has been said so far that the approach to political institutions must be guided by the wish to discover how far they canalize informed judgment into harmonizing behaviour, and what are their effects on the development of informed judgment. Implicit is the real case for representative government. For the citizen to share in the choice of those who are to run the state and in the determination of the policy they are to adopt is to make, in that measure, the activities in which he participates as a citizen the reflection of his own judgment. His behaviour, instead of being the result of external compulsion, is in that degree the application in practice of his own *weltanschauung*. It has meaning for him and contributes to the fulfilment of his personality because it fits into his scheme of things. It is purposive and not reflexive. It has moral content inasmuch as it is willed by himself in conformity with his personal moral ideal. Fundamentally the democratic claim rests on the fact that conscious willing alone gives moral meaning to activity and that happiness is conditioned by it.

But if the principle of the greatest possible degree of conscious control of activity applies to the internal organization of the state, so does it to all other collectivities. The state being only one form of association among many, other associations also are to be judged by the same test. There is no room within a democratic society for an authoritarian party, economic undertaking, church, or trade union. Each association existing to serve the purposes of those who take part in it must be determined in its actions by the definition of purpose made by its members. For the more conscious is each that the collective will is his own the more does his own activity in fulfilment of it as an active member of the association conduce to his own realisation of himself. A party which does not permit the free expression of opinion within its ranks, or provide for the determination of policies by its membership is not in conformity with the principles of democracy. For a body designed to encourage the abdication of judgment is inimical to them. By discouraging reflection and personal responsibility it is developing a habit of mind inconsistent with the good life. The principle on which self-government within the state is based, if it is sound for that organization, is valid also for a church, trade union, or economic enterprise. The principle which justifies the citizen's claim to a share in the control of his own actions as that control issues in state policy must apply to his actions as an employee of a public, or of a private, enterprise. A doctrine which instructs a man to accept moral principles because of their origin, or to resign his will in favour of 'revelation', by insisting that there is no need for him to think out rationally an integration of his own experience, denies the foundation of morality and teaches him habits which inhibit its development in him. Maximum conformity between conscious social direction and the actions so directed means consultation at every point of possible divergence and a flowing together of opinions to produce as real a collective judgment as the differences of circumstance permit.

The need being to maximize the voluntary type of action in accordance with the consciousness of shared responsibility, primacy attaches to the persuasive and educational sides of collective activity. Compulsion is secondary, whether it be the state or an economic undertaking which is in question. This means that in every function the first object is to persuade. The first task is that of the political leader or the public relations officer, not of the dictator or bureaucrat. At every point at which the state touches the citizen the aim is voluntary collaboration. Explanation and persuasion are essential elements in public administration, the official being a leader in co-operation rather than an autocrat; an agent of the community which it is his business to serve rather than a figure clothed in state omnipotence with a policeman at his elbow.

It means, to take an illustration from economic life, that the principle needs to be applied at different levels in such an organization as a nationalized coal industry. In the first place, this can be regarded as an enterprise to convert a particular kind of social property to social use, and society as a whole is naturally concerned to see that the most efficient service is provided, to co-ordinate it with other services, to secure continuity and development, to ensure suitable standards, and so on. The person working in the industry, whether as employer, official, manager, miner, salesman, or anything else, is concerned as a citizen in all this, but as a citizen is no more and no less concerned than other citizens however remote from the industry. Social policy controlling the operations of the industry reflects social purpose in which he shares, and the more directly he is conscious of sharing in it the better. That is one important argument for organizing systematic accountability to the public for the operation of the industry. The more vital it is to the life of the community, or the more liable it is to be submitted to control rendered relatively irresponsible by monopolistic development, the stronger is this argument.

But the person working in the industry is also joined in a different set of co-operative relationships confined to his function as a producer. Here too the same considerations apply. Although this association represents a narrower aspect of his social context, with a purpose which, because it is more restricted, is subordinate to the wider purpose he shares as a member of society, nevertheless as an association it also needs to ensure that its policy shall reflect the collective purpose of its members, that they shall contribute their informed judgment to the decisions it makes, and shall be aware of such decisions as a rational and open process, that is to say as responsibly taken and capable of reasoned justification. For it is no less needful in this narrower form of association that men should be conscious of the policy which controls and directs their actions as a rational and disinterested process in which, according to their function and ability, they share, and that their activity in conformity with it accordingly represents an application of their own consciousness. Indeed, so much of a man's life is spent in this kind of activity that it is here, where he is co-operatively joined with others in earning his living, that it is most important that this principle should be applied. Here too is the greatest opportunity for training in self-government. While it used to be argued that the parish and the local area afforded the foundations of democratic responsibility, and that no state could flourish as a temperate and mature political structure unless it were grounded in habits learnt around the village pump or in the parish hall, to these may even more forcibly be added today—in the changed conditions of economic and social life and of the organization of production—the factory and the workshop.

Such development corresponds too both to the demands that are increasingly made by those concerned, still more to a need of which they are often inarticulately conscious, and to the necessity that institutions should express the realities of power in actual operation. What used to be called guild socialism or workers' control is entering more urgently into the field of political institutional problems although, paradoxically, much less is now heard of it. The demand for a share in determining not only the conditions, but also the policy of the enterprise, in which they work is, of course, a long-standing one. More, it is the inevitable consequence of men's natural wish for a share in controlling what most affects them. It has become more important for several reasons, although trade unions have tended to give less expression to it owing to their preoccupation with their original purpose of securing better pay and treatment by collective bargaining and to their fear also of taking on responsibilities that might conflict with this. In the first place, the increase of knowledge, social maturity, and capacity for collective responsibility among workers, with the growth of an educated democracy, has made them more capable of sharing in control and more aware of the case for it. Again, the tremendous growth in the power of their organizations in the

DEMOCRATIC POLITICAL THEORY: APPLICATIONS 203

economic and political spheres has carried with it a responsibility for the efficiency of economic enterprise which they cannot evade save at their own cost as well as that of the community. For indeed, the greater their success in winning a bigger proportion of the product of industry the less is their chance of improvement without ensuring greater productivity. They have thus a larger stake in efficiency. The development of machinery of industrial consultation is an acknowledgment of this changing situation. So is governmental consultation of trade union organizations in the planning of economic policy, and the appointment of trade union officials to important posts in the nationalized industries. But all this, while it goes some way, is wholly inadequate to meet the real needs.

Several methods have been proposed from time to time for meeting them. The earlier ones looked to the entrusting of an industry to the workers in it, and one form of this was the proposal for the direct representation of workers on the boards of nationalized industries, either as a majority or a minority of such boards. But since this would mean that such representatives would have a divided responsibility—for efficiency to the public through Ministers and Parliament; for conditions to their constituents, the workers themselves—it had obvious dangers and disadvantages and was not favoured by the trade unions themselves. The more ambitious schemes attempted in Germany in 1919 and embodied in Article 165 of the Weimar Constitution, culminating in the State Economic Council, were over-ambitious and premature and suffered from lack of authority. But at least they made some attempt to meet the real need for they were built on the idea of partnership at workshop level extending upwards in a pyramidal structure designed to secure consultation, representation, and sharing in decision at regional and central levels too. And it is significant that a one-time guild socialist like G. D. H. Cole should lay similar emphasis on the need for organizing such partnership from the bottom upwards in British industrial life of the 1950's. As he says, the need for workers' responsibility is unanswerable. 'The case for such participation, at all levels, is that industry can be carried on efficiently, save by slave-driving methods which are now ruled out, only by inducing the workers to accept responsibility for helping to make it efficient, and that they cannot be induced to do this unless they are given due recognition as human beings entitled to a say in working arrangements and policies which intimately affect their happiness and well-being.'[1] 'Workers' control, at the workshop level, means that the workers, instead of labouring under the orders of foremen and supervisors appointed from above, will work as a group, appointing their own production leaders and accepting a collective responsibility for the organization of the work and for output.' Such a principle of organization has its obvious structural applications at the higher levels too, and by it alone can the consciousness of a shared purpose and control be made to give a fuller meaning to their activities. By it alone, increasingly in modern conditions, can the requirements of efficient production be met.

But it is not only the needs of production which are involved. The case lies deeper, in the need that individual personality be recognized and promoted, in the conditions of self-realization, happiness, 'the good life'. It belongs, that is to say, to the foundations of democratic political theory. For these, if they are valid at all, are valid for any society, for a group joined together in the context of industry no less than in a wider political context, or indeed in any other context.

Their implication is that political structure must necessarily be federal and complex. Because all people belong to several groups or societies, in which they are joined by community of interest or one kind or another, and because in each the personal fulfilment of its members is a relevant test of justification, we can say that society as a whole is by nature plural, and the relationships within it necessarily federal.

What makes a society is the fact that its members are conscious of being one. Their sense of community rests on awareness of common interests and purpose, based on common experience and beliefs. It is this also which creates obligation.[2] The common factor—which may be vocational, ethnic, regional, national, or something else—both unites the members to one another and distinguishes them from the rest of the world. But other common factors combine the same people in different ways; and there is always a larger society to which they

[1] G. D. H. Cole, *An Introduction to Trade Unionism* (1953), p. 284.
[2] See above, p. 72.

also in some measure belong; until we reach the ultimate of international society, or mankind. This also has some things in common, as well as the many that in the past have served to divide. Of the former it is not too much to assert that there is an increasing awareness of their existence, and consequently of their overriding claim.

The conditions of unity in such diversity constitute a practical political problem of prime importance. To its solution political theory can properly be expected to be a guide. For this it cannot be content with a 'value-free' description of behaviour or account of the institutions through which behaviour is given regularity, even if it could ever cheat itself into believing that this had been attained On the contrary, it must seek the pattern of purpose which gives them meaning and form. That is to say it must explain activity and institutions in terms of the motive forces giving them direction or the objectives at which they aim. It must analyse the relationship between ends and means, and suggest grounds for pronouncing upon the validity of the one and the efficiency of the other. Thus it has to consider questions relating to social purpose, asking both what men want out of life in society, and how their wants get themselves expressed in a body of moral principles constituting terms of a system of co-operation. The idea of obligation to this system derives solely and directly from the wants it is designed to meet. The unity of purpose it expresses is a rational structure; its claim to acceptance as such a unity being based on reasoned inferences, on the one hand from common wants to common instrumentalities of satisfaction, on the other from acknowledged diversity to agreed ways of settling the conflicts to which diversity leads. For an agreed means of settlement is also a common want.

INDEX

Aquinas, 31, 47
Aristotle, 11, 33, 42, 48, 62, 127, 163, 165
Augustine, 11
Authoritarian attitudes, 71, 133, 140
Authority, as absolute, 18–19, 99–100, 137, 139–40, 193
    fear of, 84
    from agreed ends, 61–3, 72, 93, 169
    from reasoned acceptance, 71, 100, 140

Bacon, F., 51
Bagehot, W., 113
Bentham, 28, 50, 53, 54, 55, 98, 101, 111
Bosanquet, 11, 17, 20
Buddhism, 125
Burke, 16, 20
Butler, Bishop, 49, 99

Carlyle, 24, 91
Change, 20–1, 170–1
Church, 16, 17, 31–2, 44, 200
Clifford, W. K., 82
Cole, G. D. H., 203–4
Coleridge, S. T., 24
Conflict, 47, 52–3, 72, 111–12, 113, 116–17, 139–40, 205
Conscious direction, 46–7, 59, 69, 71, 75, 78–9, 84–6, 89, 101, 152, 160, 167, 169, 170, 178, 181, 193, 200, 203–4
    see also Reason and behaviour, Good life
Co-operation, conditions of, 43, 52, 111–12, 123, 182–4
    institutions of, 43, 52, 111–12, 138–40, 154, 170, 182, 201, 205
    need for, 109, 111

and order, 14, 117, 201
    see also State
Criteria, political, 31–41, 168–70, 179, 198

Democracy, 67, 74, 169, 172–87, 198, 205
    see also State
Determinism, 90–2, 143, 152–3, 154–5
Dewey, J., 68, 69, 76, 81, 138, 144, 147–50

Education, 89, 114, 160, 165, 192–4
Equality, 116, 124, 128, 138–9, 172, 173, 185, 186
Esher, Viscount, 72
Eysenk, Prof., 40

Federalism, *see* Plural society
Figgis, 32
Flugel, J. C., 69, 114
Freedom, 124, 126, 128, 131, 138–9, 183, 188–90
Freud, S., 80, 84
Froude, H., 54

Ginsberg, Prof. M., 16, 41, 43, 44, 95, 106–7, 108, 186
Good life, 42–9, 70, 78, 97, 104, 138, 139, 161, 163, 167, 181, 183, 193, 195, 200
    and conscious direction, 46, 78, 104–5, 161, 181, 189–91, 200
    and happiness, 46, 49, 101, 161, 167, 204
    as harmony of ideal and practice, 46–8, 77–9, 167, 173, 205
    and individual valuations, 45–7, 70, 79, 97, 101, 138, 160
    needs and, 43–7, 83, 111, 154–5, 163, 187, 195, 205

and political purpose, 42, 138, 183
and reason, 78, 101, 167, 181, 185, 193–5
and social valuation, 104, 111, 118, 138, 185, 204
see also morality, reason and behaviour
Good, social, 22, 119, 141–55
Green, T. H., 19, 33, 41, 47, 48, 80, 86, 102–3, 104–5, 107, 125, 141, 160, 170

Hampshire, S., 138
Harding, Prof. D. W., 109, 129, 130, 147
Happiness, 48, 49–60, 75–6, 87, 101, 124, 138, 140, 160, 161, 170
   greatest, principle, 56, 58, 61, 140, 157
Hare, R. M., 62, 63, 64
Hegel, 11, 16, 21, 24
Hitler, 126, 127, 174, 184
Hobbes, 16, 22, 28
Hobhouse, L. T., 33, 41, 43, 47, 50, 51, 77, 78, 79, 86, 104–5, 185
Hobson, J. A., 142, 154
Hume, 62, 108, 127

Individual judgment, 66–7, 76, 87–8, 90, 115, 132, 133, 137, 141, 143–4, 146, 178
   and state, 24, 45, 54, 90, 129–34, 138, 142–3, 145–6, 152–3, 160, 169
International society, 205
   see also United Nations, War

Jouvenel, B. de., 43

Kant, 19, 99

Laski, H. J., 33, 41, 47, 108, 141, 161, 189
Leisure, 143, 163–4, 165
Lenin, 153
Lindsay, Lord, 11, 29
Locke, J., 108, 117, 190

Lovejoy, A. O., 137

Macbeath, Prof. A., 187
MacTaggart, J. M. E., 51
Marx, 11, 80, 91, 159
Mayhew, H., 136
McDougall, W., 142
Mill, J. S., 37, 41, 53, 76, 127, 131, 150, 158, 160, 165, 172, 175, 189
Money-Kyrle, R. E., 161
Moore, Prof. G. E., 33, 127, 151
Morality, as absolute, 94, 96, 119, 123, 125, 132–3, 137, 139–40, 148–9, 181, 200
   and reason, 48, 58, 59, 64–73, 94–139, 144–5, 153, 161, 168–9, 199
   and state, 17–20, 43
Morris, W., 160

Needs, 45–6, 83–7, 108–12, 115, 118, 128, 140, 151, 154–5, 160, 164, 165, 168, 177, 186, 195, 205
Neurosis, 162–3, 165

Obedience, 17, 24, 33, 157, 184, 196–7
Obligation, 17, 22, 61–72, 107, 111, 182–7, 204, 205
Owen, R., 160

Parties, 41, 200
Personality, fulfilment of, 44, 45
   see also Responsibility
Pieper, J., 143
Plato, 33, 62, 77, 78, 126, 127
Pleasure, 49–59, 87, 103, 110, 151, 166
   of benevolence, 54–5, 110
Plural society, 117, 204–5
Prior, Prof. A. N., 38
Property, 124, 128, 129, 190–2
Psycho-analysis, 68, 69, 71–2, 161–2
Psychology, 40, 42, 71, 83, 107, 144–5, 152

Reason, abstract, 19, 47, 67, 81–2, 97, 133

INDEX

and behaviour, 46–9, 59, 64–73, 74–92, 98, 100–2, 111, 118–40, 149–52, 161, 167, 168–9, 173, 178, 180, 193, 195–6, 202, 205
Rees, Prof. J. C., 32, 36, 37, 75
Religion, 128, 129, 134–7
Repression, 84–5
Responsibility, personal, 84–6, 139, 158, 159–61, 164, 169, 194, 195, 200, 204
Revolution, 21
Ricardo, 158, 159
Russell, Bertrand, 66, 112, 146
Ryle, Prof. G., 78, 81

Self, realization
    see also Good life, personal fulfilment, conscious direction, happiness, responsibility, reason and behaviour
Selfishness, 52–3, 54, 56, 59, 110, 151
Sidgwick, H., 54, 58, 156, 157
Sin, 12, 68, 70, 194
Slavery, 124, 191
Smith, Adam, 99
Socialism, 158, 159–60, 192, 201, 203
Spencer, H., 11, 40, 90, 98, 101, 108
Spinoza, 49, 76, 86
Sprott, Prof. W. J. H., 47
Stalin, 126, 127
State, an association, 11, 15, 16, 26, 32, 115, 118, 157, 182, 200
    common ends, 14, 39–41, 48, 61–2, 72, 89, 97, 114–15, 117, 118–19, 155, 180, 197, 204–5
    as co-operative organizations, 14, 43, 48, 57–8, 72, 74, 89, 97, 110, 112–17, 118–19, 138–40, 154, 181–3, 186, 192, 196, 198, 201

and force, 12, 14, 27, 131–2, 140, 157
limitations on, 12–14, 129–32, 182
metaphysical, 16–27, 29, 47, 67, 102, 151
mystical view of, 16–27, 29, 47, 67, 102, 151
nature of, 11, 157
purpose of, 12, 14, 28, 31, 32–3, 37, 42–60, 61, 74, 78, 118–19, 155, 156–70, 179, 185, 196, 200, 205
traditions and, 15, 32, 112–15, 131, 136, 141–2, 198
welfare, 15, 159, 192

Tawney, Prof. R. H., 40, 165
Temple, William, Archbishop, 59
Tolerance, 133
Toulmin, Prof. S., 112
Toynbee, Prof., 40
Trade Unions, 17, 32, 200, 202–3
Truman, President, 65

United Nations, 11, 12, 13
Utilitarianism, 46, 50–60, 148, 154, 158, 159

Values, patterns of, 126, 129, 131, 134–40, 142, 150, 153–5, 166, 178, 205
Violence, 184, 187–8

Walker, K., 84, 85, 142
Wallas, Graham, 78
War, 113, 125
    see also International, conflict
Weldon, T. D., 33, 34, 39, 62, 67, 68
Westermarck, 95, 97–102
Will, general, 19–20
    real, 19–20, 22
Woolf, L., 126–7, 193